Sacred Space

The Art of Sacred Silence, Sacred Speech, and The Sacred Ear in the Echo of the Still Small Voice of God

John D. Duncan

Austin Brothers Publishing
Fort Worth, Texas

© 2014 by John D. Duncan

Sacred Space: The Art of Sacred Silence, Sacred Speech, and
The Sacred Ear in the Echo of the Still Small Voice of God
by John D. Duncan
ISBN 978-0-9903477-4-3

Published by Austin Brothers Publishing
Fort Worth, Texas
www.austinbrotherspublishing.com

Printed in the United States of America

This and other books published by
Austin Brothers Publishing can be purchased at
www.austinbrotherspublishing.com

Contents

Foreword

Get ready to be restored. John Duncan is going to take you on his journey of "stopping to start." In the middle of his very active and prolific life, John does what many people in their midlife times dream of doing. He stops to rest, reflect, listen, praise, muse, and, yes, write.

In some ways, John Duncan is like most of us. We also have occasionally felt that in the middle of our busy schedules we have somehow, as Dante so famously puts it, found ourselves in a dark wood and the road is gone. In other ways, John is unique in his special combination of a pastor's heart, involved in shepherding large numbers of people, a scholar's disposition, in acquiring a Ph.D. at Cambridge, and a poet's soul, in savoring the beauty of a Texas dawn or a Blue Ridge evening.

To be honest, some books I scan. I started reading John's book as I rode on a crowded subway with people shoving each other and shouting in order to get into the door of the car. I slowed down as I continued to read John's book. I suppose that is part of his point. One of the things I noticed was John's vulnerability, as he talked about his change in life and his musing on the possible failure and success of his own actions. Another thing I saw was what I understood as his deep reading, absorbing writers as various as Rilke and Hemingway, and placing their comments in the context of God. It's clear that he is not just quoting some other contemporary Christian writer with another sound bite. He has read these books and has taken them seriously.

A third thing that comes out effortlessly in his writing is his deep love and knowledge of the Bible, and his own background studying the Greek and Roman context of the New Testament. Finally, John's tender pastoral care for people that he loves bleeds through, even when he is talking of something else.

My own experiences with John color my view. He was a pastor of a church that partners with our work with those that are homeless or in difficult situations in New York City. In his time, the church not only continued their phenomenal help, but also became a major part of a new center that provided, in a faith context, legal services and other services to those who are in one of the most challenging areas in the city. Through his visits we became friends, and I saw in him a secret yearning for something more. I saw an adventure ahead of him.

You will read about his adventure, both external and internal, and perhaps find in yourself that secret yearning for something more, a movement from a busy life to a quiet whole life, a movement from mere activity to something different. He calls it a *sacred space*.

Get ready. In its own quiet way, this is a dangerous book. Don't say I didn't warn you.

Taylor Field
Pastor Director
Graffiti Church
NYC

Introduction

I write from Cambridge, England. As I write the temperature holds at sixty-one degrees Fahrenheit. September fades and October arrives in a few days. Already crispness vibrates in the Cambridge morning air. Leaves have begun their process of changing colors. The beautiful green leaves are now outlined with yellow edges. Falling leaves float effortlessly in the air as a gentle breeze blows. Fallen leaves provide a carpet for the walking paths below my feet.

Cambridge thrives as a university town, but symbolizes Everyman or Everywoman in almost any town, city, or nook and cranny of the earth. Earlier today I walked near King's College in front of the Copper Kettle restaurant. Walking, I saw a young, tall, handsome, over-technologized man coming toward me. He talked, of course, on his cell phone. He seemed rushed, incensed, and harried.

As he drew closer he appeared agitated, the inflection of his voice rising and falling as I overheard part of his phone conversation. Obviously, he had just returned from London. I did pick up that much of his speech. Also, he indicated his lateness for an appointment or important meeting. Then, in animated fashion, his facial expression more relaxed than it had been, he uttered the words I will never forget, "It was like trying to move sheep across London Bridge."

The expression I had never heard before. The vivid image painted pictures in my brain: of sheep stuck on London Bridge, or of an agitated man stuck in a cab that did not move on London Bridge, or of a slow moving British rail system that delayed his valued time, or of the slow moving paperwork in the Cambridge University system, or finally, maybe sheep lazily moving across London Bridge did snarl traffic and made the young man snarky? Do sheep still move across London Bridge in the 21st century? Do you ever feel bottle-necked, overloaded, trapped?

Do sheep still move across *London Bridge* **in the 21st century? Do you ever feel bottle-necked,** *overloaded,* **trapped?**

One thing for certain, my anonymous friend filtered through the Cambridge crowd in cramped space, hurried, harried, and agitated. The world had slowed down and the sheep brought his life to a slow crawl or a standstill or, at the least, the world bottlenecked at an inopportune time. The result was agitation, frustration, and perturbed words at the crossroads and in the rush to the next big thing, whatever it was.

A wise sage once described the hectic pace of life in three words: hurry, worry, and bury. Richard Foster in *Celebration of Discipline* acknowledges, "In contemporary society our Adversary majors in three things: noise, hurry, and crowds."[1] Alvin Toffler prophesied in *Future Shock* (1970) a future society shocked and unnerved by too much change in a short period of time. He theorized a condition in society where "information overload," as he coined the phrase, would overpower individuals to create overarching stress and disorientation.

My anonymous friend hurriedly walking through Cambridge while chatting on his cell phone symbolizes the stress and disorientation that has arrived at our doorsteps and interrupted our hearts at peace. Hurry, worry, and crowds, if you will, hyper-charged with cell phones and a frantic racehorse pace, and my anonymous friend as a symbol, remind me that sacred space and a

---

1 Richard J. Foster, *Celebration of Discipline: The Path to Spiritual Growth* (2nd ed.; New York, New York: Harper and Row, Publishers, 1988), 15.

sacred heart might not be championed today. Still, sacred space is absolutely necessary for the sacred heart.

Everywhere, from the streets of Cambridge to a restaurant in Chicago to an airport in Atlanta to a museum in New York to a church in Los Angeles, in homes, in work space, in cars, in stores, in fast food lines, and in grocery stores-all over the world, information overload burdens and pushes aside a sense of the sacred.

Several years ago I traveled to London by train to explore the city and, especially, Westminster Abbey. When I take the train to London from Cambridge I take everything in: the rolling hills filled with green landscape and cascading hills of grain at certain times of the year; people working the fields, cars, bikes, villages, church steeples, people on the train listening to their iPods, reading iPads or books, and the annoying person talking on his or her cell phone. Arriving in London as the fast train slows to a crawl the city comes alive with tall buildings, boats on the River Thames, and hurried people buzzing like bees in a hive.

One particular day when I traveled to London, I maneuvered through the train station and through the tube system amid "Mind the Gap," noise of conversations galore, and the fast pace of people much like the fast train I just exited. I then made way to Westminster Abbey. The towering church in the shadow of British Parliament and the clock Big Ben not too far from the huge Ferris wheel known as the London Eye intrigued me. The church as a place of worship and an intern for famous corpses and crypts seemed eerie, but nonetheless inviting as curiosity sometimes overpowers misgivings.

I paid the entry fare and purposely sought out the crypts of kings and queens while paying special attention to poet's Corner in the south transept of the abbey. I noted poets commemorated like Kipling, Lord Byron, Browning, and Alfred Lord Tennyson as well as literary icons like Dickens, Dr. Samuel Johnson, Henry James, and Geoffrey Chaucer.

Of particular notice and interest to me was the memorial stone of Gerard Manley Hopkins (1844-1889), the priest and poet whose mysticism, melancholy, and rhythmic poetry astonishes me both in melodic flow to ignite my imagination and in mystical fire to inspire my soul. I can almost hear Hopkins's imaginative voice in my mind uttering..."Glory be to God for dappled things" or

"The world is charged with the grandeur of God" or "let him Easter in us, be a dayspring to the dimness of us" or "I say that we are wound With mercy round and round As if with air" "Look at the stars! look, look up at the skies! O look at the fire-folk sitting in the air! The bright boroughs, the circle citadels there!"[2]

That last phrase, from Hopkins's poem "The Starlight Night," enraptures, but also possesses two dissonant lines: "Ah well! It is all a purchase, all is a prize. Buy then! bid then!-What!-Prayer, patience, alms, vows." The aura, beauty and grandeur of the abbey, it's transcendence with its stained glass, Christian symbols of cross and crypt (prayer, patience, alms!), marble, history, elegance, and power, as I toured seemed to contrast with the immanence of the present, the weariness of the tourists, the rush to view everything before the doors closed and the gift shop stopped selling postcards, coffee mugs, and other wares (Buy then! bid then!).

Hopkins's poem indicates the precipice on which we walk, or even fall: between transcendence and immanence; between heaven and

2 See Ryan, Thomas, *Hopkins: The Mystic Poets Series* (Woodstock, Vermont: SkyLight Paths Publishing, 2004), 1-ff.

earth; between temporal and spiritual; between good and evil, Christ and Satan; between hushed quiet (prayer, patience, alms!) and rushed consumerism (buy then! bid then! pay the fare!).

Nowhere did this struggle and reality play out any more than as I observed the abbey. People milled around near the high altar, itself a golden tower inside the abbey, a monstrosity decorated with Christian symbols and mosaics. People walked and talked, talking as the pitch of voices rose and fell and echoed off of the tall ceiling.

> **I noticed, much to my *surprise*, people walking and talking, but slipped beneath the *hubbub* of activity and echoes of *noise*, people kneeling, praying, reciting prayers to the Almighty.**

I noticed, much to my surprise, people walking and talking, but slipped beneath the hubbub of activity and echoes of noise, people kneeling, praying, reciting prayers to the Almighty. How strange, I thought, the recklessness of the tourists (buy then! bid then!) and prayers of the saints (prayers, patience, vows!) collided. In an instant as the loud noise echoed in the abbey chambers, a praying woman suddenly sprung from her knees in animated fashion, her eyebrow furled, her face furled as if angry, and grabbed a sign and held it high for all the tourists to see. The sign read: "Quiet, please!"

Is there no sacred space? No sacred silence with which to offer sacred speech and calm the ear no less sacred?

Just the other day in the check-out at the grocery store a lady echoed my sentiment, "Is nothing sacred anymore?" I have no idea exactly what she was talking about, but she might well have been standing in Westminster Abbey near the rush of closing time in the crucial hour of prayer.

Sacred, what does the word even mean? A dictionary definition tells you that sacred means "to set apart," "holy," or dedicated to the worship of a deity. If you looked up sacred in Greek you would find the word *agios*. The word means "holy." In the Bible you find words like sacred mountain, sacred temple, and the like. Even Jesus proposed a wise maxim, "Do not give what is sacred (*agios*, "holy") to the dogs, nor cast your pearls before swine" (Matthew 7:6). I would not recommend that you cast your pearls before swine, nor cast your swine before pearls, unless trust falls between real friends. Some of what we say is reserved only for the ears of one or two true friends, sacred words or sacred speech set apart for only one person. Do not give what is sacred to dogs.

The apostle Paul spoke of the body as the temple as *sacred*, "Don't you know that you yourselves are God's temple and that God's Spirit lives in you? If anyone destroys God's temple, God will destroy him; for God's temple is sacred, and you are that temple" (I Corinthians 3:16-17, *NIV*). Did you see it? God's temple, the human body set apart for

> **Some of what we say is *reserved* only for the ears of one or two true friends, sacred words or sacred speech *set apart* for only one person. Do not give what is *sacred* to dogs.**

God, remains sacred.

If you look up *sacred* in Latin the gamut runs wild from *sacra* or *sacer* (sacred) to *sacerdotalis* (priestly) to *sacramentum* (an oath and guarantee or deposit of money in a lawsuit) to *sacrarium* (shrine, chapel, sacred place) to *sacrificium*

(sacrifice) to *sacrilegium* (sacrilege; temple robbing, violation of sacred rites). What is sacred requires value, a pledge or oath to its value, and a sacrificial element, holding nothing back if you will, giving your all to it, as if your life depended on it. To violate or to demonstrate violence toward the sacred proves sacrilegious, a kind of temple robbing, and definite violation of sacred rites.

In antiquity the Roman concept of sacra combined two ideas: first, in a religious sense of homage to a god or family sacred rites, an oath or pledge, especially in honor of burial for a relative; two, in a legal sense, sacra later connected to Roman law in legal inheritance, legal rights passed from one generation to the next. In a religious sense, Romans in antiquity pledged to their god or deity by giving up something or removing something from their presence like a bull, piece of bread, cake, or wine. The sacrifice ("to make sacred") was then made to the god on the altar by sacrificing the bull, leaving the bread at the altar, placing the cake on the altar, or pouring the wine over the altar. A religious act involved a sacred act.

In a legal sense an oath spoken and translated as a binding obligation became a part of the family folklore, legal inheritance, and legal rights transferred.

In simplest terms, what was sacred demanded three things: a pledge or oath of homage and honor; a commitment to follow through on obligations to the deity, god or family inheritance; and sacrificial acts to follow through on what a person deemed sacred. What is sacred is religious, valued, set apart, focused in my life. What is sacred is personal but also passed on, shared, a passport for life and witness in a life joyfully lived. What is sacred is binding, a personal obligation not ignored by the life I choose and hope to live under the shadow of God's wings and in the air of His grace.

Standing in Westminster Abbey that day and even writing now, I gain a strong feeling for the sacred as honor to Christ by an oath or pledge of commitment, a commitment to follow through as a follower of Christ, and sacrificial elements set apart in my life.

Standing in Westminster Abbey that day and even writing now I am torn between buy now, bid then! and prayers, patience, vows!; between sacrifice and the sacrilegious; between temple honor and temple robbing; between setting apart the sacred and throwing that which is sacred to the dogs.

Standing in the Westminster Abbey that day and writing now I find myself struggling with a sense of church: the sacredness of the towering steeple church called the abbey in its glory and grandeur as a temple of worship to the Almighty and the place where consumers shop and search to have their own needs met while casually

A society that refuses *Sabbath* restfulness for all is bound to fail...

walking, talking, and texting their friends; transcendence and imminence; heaven and earth; the spiritual and the temporal, so to speak.

I must confess, if I have not already, that solving the age old dilemmas of transcendence and immanence or the spiritual and temporal or religious sacrifice and consumer wants is not my aim in writing this book. I am caught in all this discussion between rest and restlessness as much as any person like tourist waltzing through Westminster Abbey. I tend to agree with Walter Brueggemann. He says, "If performed Sabbath does not in reality break the pattern of restless acquisitiveness, trouble will come. A society that refuses Sabbath restfulness for all is bound to fail..."[3]

Substitute "the sacred" for "Sabbath" and you will see why I write this book. I believe a restless society needs to reclaim the sacred to find rest. I believe trouble looms on the horizon as if the abbey ceiling falls down or the high altar decays and crumbles unless we give time to sacred space. I believe that churches, but more importantly, Christians, need to slow down and make room for sacred space to renew their vision for life and their enthusiasm for living for Christ. Lastly and most importantly, I write this book because the damaged soul can only find renewal when time given to the sacred opens hearts and minds to the joy of Christ.

I give you disclaimers as I write and as you read. My soul has been damaged; by an overloaded schedule; an over-technologized mind that pushed aside time for the sacred; and an over-hyped consumer church that marginalized what I valued as sacred: Christ, the cross and the resurrection. I fear that my schedule devalued time

---

3 Walter Brueggemann, *Sabbath as Resistance: Saying No to the Culture of Now* (Louisville, Kentucky, 2014), 67.

alone with God. I fear that many of my parishioners whom I pastored frantically busied themselves with life that they missed Life, the Christ-Life. I fear that the church I served as pastor/ undershepherd put their faith in programs, plans, and purposes contrary to the cross rather than faith in the Good Shepherd. Come to think of it, at times I had done the same.

And so, I guess, I write for healing: for me, the people of God, and for the church. How can we find rest in the restlessness? How can we experience peace in a storm tossed sea of trouble? How can we discover the sacred among the mundane, temporal things of earth?

After all, I know what we have to have on earth, pay the bills, take the kids to soccer, show up for work, send texts, send pictures to friends, and take vacations, even tour towering cathedrals. I know duty calls, stress builds like a volcano, and pressures to perform daily tasks threaten the soul's survival. I know the challenges of work and play, faith and family life, dreams long hoped for and the sorrow of a dream buried in despair and seeming hopelessness.

I know of a place, quiet, personal, and real to me. The space is sacred, hallowed, and precious.

The place sits deep in the mountains of North Carolina in a mining town not far from the highest peak east of the Mississippi River, Mount Mitchell. Once upon a time a garden sprawled with luscious food from the earth: corn, green beans, potatoes, and cabbage. On each side of the house once upon a time trees stood erect, straight up with limbs towering and as significant to me as the steeple of Westminster Abbey to picture-taking tourists.

> **I fear that my schedule *devalued* time alone with God.**

Facing the house to the left, a spruce pine tree stood its sweeping branches like brooms and its sweet smell at certain times of the year heightens the olfactory senses in the nose to pleasantness. On the right of the house stood an apple tree dropping fruit galore when the branches were shaken. What sacred space does to the soul invites us to slow down, stop the hurry and worry and push away from the noise and technology to focus on Christ in His sweetness and Christ in fruitfulness.

By the way, on the porch of the house, white and pointed in an A-frame, but dwarfed by spruce pine, maple, and apple trees, hangs a green swing on the porch where I encounter sacred space. While I have a *place* in North Carolina, sacred space to shut the world out for minutes, hours, days and renew my soul in Christ, what I propose here is not so much a place like that, but finding daily renewal, sacred space wherever you live and move and have your being. It is essential to avoid trouble. It is vital for the soul to find balance in life. It is critical for your journey in life and absolutely necessary for spiritual health as a follower of Jesus.

So I write to share with you, not so much a place, but a way of the heart and mind and soul, a way to enter sacred space and rediscover Christ's freshness and renewal for life. C. S. Lewis said, "The central Christian belief is that Christ's death has somehow put us right with God and given us a fresh start."[4] I wish to help you find the right and embrace the fresh in the shadow of the Almighty.

How will I do this? Chapter one discusses sacred silence, what the Greeks named *euphemia*,

---

4 C. S. Lewis, *The Case for Christianity* (New York, NY: Touchstone, 1996), 46

as a doorway from noise to quiet. Chapter two will highlight sacred speech, what is known as *proseuxomai*, a Jewish concept of prayer that moves from the soul from chaos to peace. Chapter three will focus upon the sacred ear, the Greek concept of *akouo*, "acoustics," as a path to listen to God and move from a soul in exile to a soul of purpose.

Even on days when I am not in the mountains of North Carolina I find myself in the green swing, a gentle breeze blowing, the swing swaying, my head rested on a pillow, daydreaming, talking to God, and renewing my soul by means of sacred space. Join me as we enter into sacred space. Turn the page and explore sacred silence as the first step to sacred space.

Sacred Silence
From Noise to Quiet

"Humility seeks silence not in inactivity but in ordered activity, in that activity that is proper to our poverty and helplessness before God."

~Thomas Merton, *Thoughts on Solitude*[5]~

---

5 Thomas Merton, *Thoughts on Solitude* (New York, New York: Farrar, Straus and Giroux, 1958), 88.

My right ear hurts. I went to the doctor. He pulled on my ear. He picked up his otoscope, turned on the small light, and looked in my ear. He pushed around the outer rim of the hole in my ear leading to the ear drum and groaned.

"Yep," he said, "You have an outer ear infection. Now it's not an inner ear infection, but an outer ear infection. I will give you some ear drops, one for the infection and one for the pain. The pain will subside in a couple of days."

He left the room and returned after a lengthy delay. My ear hurt even worse after he pulled on it. I guess the infection arrived in my ear from too much time swimming in blue ocean waters at Atlantis Beach. I will take a pain in the ear any day for my time at the beach.

This was not the first time I had been to the doctor because of my right ear. I am not hearing too well in this ear. Once I had an emergency visit to the doctor because a small spider climbed in my ear, traversed down the opening, down the ear tubes to the ear drum. Imagine two things: the tickling sensation that nearly drove me crazy, and the sound of my eardrum drumming like the sound of a drummer in a band swishing cymbals in a musical piece.

It happened in my ear. I reacted. I instinctively stuck my finger in my ear and squashed the critter. When the doctor retrieved the spider's legs, he explained the spider theory and what happens when a spider enters the ear cave. I experienced it.

When the spelunking spider entered my ear it slid down into my ear cavities. The human ear fascinates me. Your ear comprises three sections: an inner, middle, and an outer ear. The outer ear can be seen as what might be described as ears, small, large, flappy, full of cartilage, and covered by skin that then weaves its way down an s-shaped canal about one and one-half inches long. Hairs grow there and protect the ear. Wax also forms in that part of the ear.

The middle ear contains the tympanic membrane or eardrum along with mastoid bone, and the Eustachian tube that connects to the nasal pharynx that is affected when you yawn or swallow. Next in line are the auditory ossicles or ear bones. We learn in high school science about the hammer, anvil, and stirrup in the ear that transmit vibrations from the ear drum to the inner ear.

The inner ear comprises the semicircular canal that possesses fluid and helps you keep your equilibrium and balance. The inner ear opens from the vestibule into the cochlea which translates as the acoustic branch and nerve center which sends vibrations, sound, and impulses to the brain. When the spider jettisoned my ear and I heard sound, this nerve center activated sound, in a sense, and transmitted what I heard, and sometimes do not hear clearly, into my ear.

In the 21st century the human ear appears overworked, hyper-sensitized, and stimulated beyond reason. Did you know that you can download an app on your cell phone that measures decibels of sound? If you listen to loud music at 95 decibels or more over extended periods of time it expedites hearing loss. A jet engine, a gun when fired, and heavy equipment like a weed eater, lawnmower, sandblaster, or motorcycle fires at such elevated decibels that the government regulation suggests people using such equipment wear ear muffs, and in some cases doubly protect the ears.

Music can calm and soothe the ear, or blast your eardrum. Water cascading off a mountain into a waterfall comforts the ear. A calm wind ruffling leaves on a maple tree clams the ear. A high pitch or scream irritates the ear. Also, a fingernail scratched on a chalk board agitates the ear. A child who whines or baby who cries on an airplane un-settles the nerve center in the inner ear.

How many places have I been recently, the grocery store, shopping, driving through the neighborhood, and seen people with their person-al listening devices. Even a family of four tootling down the road in a minivan while every member of the family each had their own ear phone, or properly called "ear buds." Can we not even talk or at least listen to the same music?

Noise vibrates everywhere. I stopped at a red light at the edge of an intersection and heard the thump of the base in the car next to me while my own music blared over my Bose ste-reo. I wake up in the morning and turn on ESPN's SportsCen-ter to hear the noise

The church service *annoyed* **my ears like a spider dancing on my ear drum while losing his legs.**

of yesterday's scores. And I am alert to beeping machinery, parents yelling at their children, and even a church service I attended recently where the level must have risen to 98 decibels. Listen-ing to the sermon was not much of an option after my ears continued to ring and my cochlea and ear nerve center did its work to calm the noise storm. The church service annoyed my ears like a spider dancing on my ear drum while losing his legs.

Noise appears to be the order of the day, but noise arrives as an age old problem. Consider, if you read I Kings (1:41) noise from the city, the trumpets blaring meant that a new king would soon be crowned. However, while this appeared as good news to the inhabitants of Jerusalem it arrived as bad news to many in the house of David. When David ordered Solomon crowned as the king the noise registered as confusing. Noise might confuse and can be confusing to even the clearest of minds.

Noise might confuse you, but it might also alert or alarm you. Noise can startle like the sudden rush of wind whistling over the mountains or an alert scrawling and beeping on the television screen. Noise might arrive like the swift attack of an army, of if you read the prophets Isaiah (13:4) or Jeremiah (50:22), noise can shout like a protest in the noise of the crowd, like the rush of a mighty army, or the noise of battle, the noise of a great destruction at hand.

Once while staying at my grandmother's house in the mountains of North Carolina my heart raced, my eyes widened, and I lay still in bed after I heard a loud noise in the dining room. And another time when I heard and even saw as I looked out the window, a car shift the gravel on the road above the house, then stop, and turn off its headlamps. The noise, the stillness and scariness of the moment as the wind gently blew through the screen and lifted the curtains away from the wall, felt eerie and unnerving, alerting my senses and heightening my feeling of fear. The noise proved uneventful, but I longed for a calm stillness, not the stillness of eeriness that set my nerves on edge.

If you read the prophet Amos (5:23) there comes a time in worship to get our hearts right and to navigate our way back to the center-point of Christ. That the message becomes, "Away with the noise of your songs! I will not listen to the music of your harps." Maybe music sounds that forth notes everywhere needs to be shut off, if only for minutes or a season as we find our way back to the still small voice of God in the echo of life's loud moments.

Everywhere we turn music blares, blasts, even belches in the boom-box generation where silence seems dreadful. Voices rise, scream, yell, signaling voices of politics, religion, work, and play in the race toward success and survival. Occasionally, voices need to be tuned out and turned off, even our own. Jesus rebuked Peter, "Get behind me, Satan!"

As I write I am experiencing *afresh* **the stillness, the quietness, and** *slowness* **of life for the first time in 34 years.**

Jesus had turned and challenged Peter, "You do not have in mind the things of God, but the things of men."

Noise, loud noise, confuses and interrupts even our simplest acts of worship. Voices often keep us from experiencing the inner quiet that allows us to function spiritually and healthily in calm at the core people of faith in Christ.

As I write I am experiencing afresh the stillness, the quietness, and slowness of life for the first time in 34 years. I had long been planning to stop everything at some point in life and try my hand at writing. I published articles, had written two doctoral theses, and returned from Cambridge, England after completion of my Ph. D. in the UK. On the peak of elation on my return to Texas where I pastored, I set forth my heart and plan to pastor and focus on God's future, angling to figure out how the seeds of 34 years of pastoral work, writing, two doctorates, and life experience would bear fruit.

Shocked and stunned when I returned, two men visited with me about "my future." The climb to the top of the mountain immediately led me on a trek down into a dark valley. Apparently, while out of the country a small group of church leaders discussed my future plans.

"You either need to re-engage in the church or move forward with your plans. We are here to suggest a way that you can move forward," the men said. Although those were not their exact words, those words indicate the gist of what they proposed.

We met a second time, and I called a friend asking to borrow his ranch. For two days I prayed at the ranch and went over and over what had just happened. A roller coaster of emotions had taken me up and down, the culmination of 12 years of hard work in England and now a suggestion that

I take some time off with no tangible plan for the future.

At the ranch I remembered a man once telling me that the church would be better off with a CEO than pastor. I recalled another editor who prophesied years ago to me that I could not write and pastor at the same time. "One day," he advised, you will have to make a choice." Was this that time of choice?

All I had known, all I had given my life to included serving Christ and serving people. I loved all of it. The challenges of serving as a pastor in the 21st century prove enormous, long days with gut-wrenching decisions, and yet many joys of shepherding people to the fresh waters of God's renewing grace.

At the ranch as I pondered my future, God's plans for the future and what life might look like going forward, I opened my Bible, my thumb fixed near the middle and Psalm 45:1, "My heart is stirred by a noble theme as I recite my verses for the king: My tongue is the pen of a ready writer," and Psalm 44 of God's work in our days and Psalm 46:10, "Be still and know that He is God."

As I read these verses I thought about two other places: North Carolina and Cambridge.

Through the years my father's house in Spruce Pine, North Carolina and Cambridge, England had been places where I rested, relaxed, found peace, and created a pace to slow down, albeit sacred space for my life.

In the process of this life-changing decision to eventually teach and write, I stumbled across one of my favorite author's autobiography; Calvin Miller's *Life is Mostly Edges*. He recounted a similar decision he made years ago. Miller wrote how he

> **None of the great *saints* of the church made his or her mark by *trying harder*, only by loving [Jesus] more completely."**

learned the secret of success from a fellow struggler, that "the secret of success is not 'busianity,' it is Christianity. None of the great saints of the church made his or her mark by trying harder, only by loving [Jesus] more completely."[6]

In his book he acknowledged that the church was causing him to lose the best part of himself, which is reading, writing, and the reward

---

6 Calvin Miller, *Life is Mostly Edges: A Memoir* (Nashville, Tennessee: Thomas Nelson, 2008), 266.

of serving Christ in that mix. His words resonated, "...it became clear to me that if I was going to save the best part of soul, it was important for me to follow God in a new direction."[7]

At the ranch I shed tears as the morning dew tickled the grass and the sun's rays cascaded over the grass covered rolling hills and the river behind the ranch house. I made my decision. I took a leap of faith. The leap has been both a deep learning experience in the jagged journey of faith and refreshing like diving into a swimming pool on a Texas summer day.

I stepped aside at the church in a leap of faith, explaining that I had written, worked, and served as pastor, and had planned to teach and write and that it was time for me to "jump in the river on a new adventure."

I left out the part about meetings because to this day the shadiness and uncomfortable feeling of thinking about those meetings still makes me sick. I never felt the three men had my best interest at heart, nor the church's. They did not ask me to leave the church, but their nudge set me on a journey I have not regretted. I understand Romans 8:28, "All things work together for good,"

---

7 Miller, *Life is Mostly Edges*, 283.

and Genesis 50:20, "God meant it for good," in exciting and pulsating rhythms afresh with adventure.

> **By January my cell phone** *stopped* **ringing, email slowed to a crawl, and** *quietness* **loomed, hovered, and even** *scared* **me.**

I even joked to a friend, "My wife and I feel like Abraham and Sarah where God said I will lead you to land that I will show you. We're not sure where he will lead, but we are praying that he does not surprise us with a baby at years of age100!"

I finished my last service on Christmas Eve, a service I love with the songs of Christmas, joy in the world, and tears. Large tears trickled down my cheeks like a waterfall on that starry night on the Christmas Eve drive home. By January my cell phone stopped ringing, email slowed to a crawl, and quietness loomed, hovered, and even scared me.

As I evaluated in January and starting writing on January 2 the first thought that occurred to me was that I had failed. The cold north winds of January and the loneliness reinforced a sense of failure. I retraced a litany of people who failed, yet ultimately succeeded: from Michael Jordan's failure to make his ninth grade basketball team to the game-changing hero of the NBA champion Chicago Bulls; from Abraham Lincoln's failed political attempts but finally rising to lead the United Sates as President in 1860; from the musician Mozart's critics to his melodious musical masterpieces; from motorcycle rider and daredevil Evil Knievel's broken bones, crashes, and unfortunate motorcycle mishaps to his grand feat of trying to jump the mile long Snake River Canyon on September 8, 1974 in a skycycle that failed because his specially designed parachute opened prematurely. At least, I thought, like Knievel I had succeeded by trying to serve, pastor, and preach.

Along the way of consoling myself, encouraging myself, working to inspire myself, and dig my way out of the doldrums I ran across an article about Eddie the Eagle.[8] "The eagle never landed," the old story goes. British Ski jumper Michael Edwards who finished last in the ski jump in the 1988 Winter Olympics in Calgary finished the Olympics as a kind of folk hero, a perennial

---

8   Franz Lidz, "The Eagle Never Landed," *Smithsonian* (February 2014): 23-7.

loveable loser. A song was written about him, "Fly Eddie, Fly." People laughed at him. He laughed at himself.

The article even quoted Eddie, a man who turned numerous failures into success by becoming a lawyer and by using his celebrity to communicate the importance of failure. Eddie the Eagle said, "To me competing was all that mattered. Americans are very much 'Win! Win! Win!' In England, we don't give a fig whether you win. It's great if you do, but we appreciate those who don't. The failures are the people who never get off their bums. Anyone who has a go is a success."[9]

I know all the quotes: "Failure is never final" and the like. Such sayings as business people often use, "you have to fail to understand success" or "failing pushes you forward" or failure clarifies the moment or life or some fretful event that feels like the bottom dropped out of your life. I even knew the stories of biblical heroes from Moses in the wilderness of Midian, to Joseph in prison, to King David on the run and in grief over sin and family turmoil, from the prophet Jeremiah in a

---

9 Franz Lidz, "The Eagle Never Landed," *Smithsonian* (February 2014): 24.

cistern, to the apostle Paul in prison yet writing a song of joy (Philippians 2:5-11).

Even G. K. Chesterton once quipped of nations, Great Britain for sure and other nations in a time of war, "But I do not believe that a nation dies by suicide. To the very last every problem is a problem of will; and if we will we can be whole. But it involves facing our failures as well as counting our successes."[10] Maybe I had to face my failings, to muster up force of will.

...the feeling of failure might actually be worse than failure itself.

For all my failings, one thing I determined: the feeling of failure might actually be worse than failure itself. Michael Jordan and Mozart and Chesterton and business gurus aside, these words and success stories often get told after success, but few people talk about the abject fear of failure or the dark side of failures' feelings. Feelings of failure often birth a twin: loneliness.

My second thought was, "This is exactly what you wanted, but it sure seems awfully lonely." I never shied away from being by myself or

---

10 Kevin Belmonte, ed., *The Quotable Chesterton: The Wit and Wisdom of G. K. Chesterton* (Nashville, Tennessee: Thomas Nelson Publishing, 2011), 75.

being alone, in fact, at times I cherished the alone time. But this felt different, a crisis of God and self and the downward spiral of loneliness's whispering ghost: "Nobody cares."

Frederick Buechner said, "To be lonely is to be aware of an emptiness that takes more than people to fill. It is to sense that something is missing which you cannot name."[11] While digging in my office for a quote on another writing project during this crisis, I stumbled across a book I had read three times, *Letters to a Young Poet* by Rainer Maria Rilke. He wrote to a poet, letters about life, freedom to encounter art in its adventure, and the struggle of the artist in both loneliness and in practicing his or her art form, in this case poetry. "We must embrace the struggle," he said. "Every living thing conforms to it. Everything in nature grows and struggles in its own way, establishing its own identity, insisting on it at all costs."[12]

Rilke advised, "Do not allow yourself to be confused in your aloneness by something within

---

11   Frederick Buechner, *Beyond Words: Daily Readings in the ABC's of Faith* (New York: HarperCollins, 2004), 226

12   Rainer Maria Rilke, *Letters to a Young Poet* (trans. Joan M. Burnham: Novato, California: New World Library, 200), 61.

you that wishes to be released from it."[13] Rilke's advice, distinguishing the loneliness and the aloneness, two clear and different words, caused me to pray and evaluate. Rilke caused me to embrace the struggle much like the apostle Paul chanted *I have fought a good fight...keep the faith or Be strong in the grace that is in Christ Jesus* (2 Timothy 4:7; 2:1).

My third revealing ponderance involved a reflective moment in despair: What had I done? Was this judgment? Blessing? Just life? Was God allowing me to focus on one or two things in an effort to free me from trying to be all things to all people all the time? Or was God sending me into a dark tunnel to thrust me into fresh light? The reflective moment actually led me into a tunnel only to emerge with a new, but bold insight. What, I thought to myself, had I changed over the years? Like a train coming down the track, one thought both startled me and encouraged me.

The revealing ponderance in the moment of despair and the one thought that emerged from the darkness was this: I had not taken time to create the sacred space in my mid-life that I did in my younger life both as a pastor and a human being.

---

13 Rilke, *Letters to a Young Poet*, 62.

Early in ministry and in my twenties and thirties I used to take days off. I would go to a friend's ranch and stay in a cabin overlooking the Brazos River in Texas all day. I would read, pray, study, and do nothing for periods of time. One fall day at the ranch I remember watching the colorful yellow and brown fading green leaves effortlessly fall off of trees and down the canyon into the slow moving river and then ease on top of the green, pea-colored water while they drifted away like rafts on a planned journey. Watching, then listening to the birds as they sang and chirped added to the drama. Occasionally, a deer or vulture afloat in the upward currents of the wind captured my eye. The silence at times offered a sacrifice of peace.

On other occasions I would take off for the mountains of North Carolina, the place I mentioned earlier in this book. The porch, alive with nature's feast of fireflies, butterflies, birds, gentle breezes, strong winds, and rain at times, provided a haven of rest. Again I read, prayed, studied, slept on the porch swing with a pillow, and listened to the silence in the sacredness of space that stilled my soul.

On other occasions I encountered Cambridge, England. Brisk walks along the River Cam in the shadow of the colleges, the array of dancing daffodils and flowers in Spring, and a bridge where I walked overlooking the punters below in the River Cam in the watchful eye of towering spires and weeping willow trees as their small leaves and long branches drooped into the waters below.

Early one morning while on a walk as the sun rose over King's College and dew kissed the morning grass, an air of freshness, and aliveness enraptured my soul as I celebrated the stillness of the morning and the sacred space God had blessed me with in that moment. The hallowedness, the holiness, the heightened sense of God, life, and the frozen frame of time that lingers in my mind even as I write provided a kind of sacred silence.

In my crisis I remembered the ranch, the porch, and the bridge as the sun rose and dew renewed the earth and my life. I realized I had gotten away from sacred space, from the timely and necessary importance of sacred silence.

One day while writing this chapter as I emerged from the dark tunnel and discovering anew the light, God spoke. I had driven home, turned into the driveway and noticed, surprisingly, two doves standing, gently in strength like soldiers standing at the front door on both sides of the walkway almost like soldiers protecting Buckingham Palace in London. At least that is what I thought at the time. The message God gave, though, falling in my heart as effortlessly as leaves tumbling down the canyon into the river, was, "Peace, be still. It will be alright. Peace. Peace be still."

My Christianity had reduced to *"busianity*," to borrow Calvin Miller's term.

I had been so busy as a pastor, racing to meetings, to the hospital, preparing to preach, chasing success like leprechauns chase gold at the end of the rainbow that I forgot to work my soul, renew my spirit, replenish my heart with things spiritual. My Christianity had reduced to "busianity," to borrow Calvin Miller's term. Confusion, noise, and worry distracted worship in my over-hyped, over technologized mind. A hyper-charged schedule overpowered my soul. Was I not like Peter? *Get behind me, Satan! You chased the things of man, but not the things of God.*

Blaise Pascal, the 17th century scientist and mathematician, once said, "All men's miseries derive from not being able to sit in a quiet room alone." Pascal, transparent and honest, also acknowledged the challenge of such quietness, "The eternal silence of these infinite spaces terrifies me."[14] Again, Pascal, in this tension between the sacred silence of the earthiness of sitting alone in a room and the terror of the infinite spaces of eternity, said, to paraphrase, "There is a God-shaped vacuum that only God can fill."

My departure from sacred space and sacred silence disconnected my soul, mind, body, and spirit. The result was frustration and the opposite of peace—turmoil, a volcanic soul spewing, burning, bubbling, boiling beneath the soul's surface ready to explode.

One simple necessity for life includes creating sacred space, a place and time alone, quiet, in a room, at a ranch, on the porch, and standing on a bridge while the rays of the sun splash your face afresh. Sacred space requires time: daily, occasional, say a day or so, or even extended time, a rest of Sabbath.

In simplest terms, we need to sit alone, focus on Christ, seek His peace. The Psalmist says, "Be still and know that He is God" (Psalm 46:10).

---

14 Blaise Pascal, *Pensées* no. 233 (1658).

Sacred space invites the weary, wounded, weak, and the strong to sit in quietness before Christ. It invites a daily routine, time set aside to sit quietly before the throne of grace where we find mercy and grace in the nick of time at the Master's feet, in the shadow of His ear, heart, and voice. Do not forget the Greek concept of *euphemia*, before praise (to God) a sacred silence is necessary. What is worthy of praise requires silence before praise, a stillness before God in His grandeur.

Sacred space sets the stage for the first step in spiritual renewal: sacred silence. The apostle Paul uses an interesting and clandestine word in Philippians 4:8. While rehearsing Christian virtue and challenging Christians to "think of these things," Paul uses the word *euphemia*, that is, "whatever things are worthy of praise."

Euphemia finds meaning in sacred silence, awe, even a sense of wonder that stops you in your tracks. The Greek philosopher Plato from Athens (c. 429-347 BC) used it in the sense of a speech you listen to, auspicious speech, that which is mind-boggling, provocative, spell-binding, that leaves you in awe.[15] *Euphemia* carries the sense of a "good report," silent thoughts of goodness

---

15 Plato, *Laws* 800.e.11.

before you share good words, or, literally, "good fame," good words about a person.[16] Even better, *euphemia* describes the silence before a sacrifice, the silence preceded by a flame of fire or silence before the high platform as the sacrifice was prepared, a moment of awe and wonder.[17] Sacred silence affirms the priority of sacred space and the first step in respect and honor to God in the wake of spiritual renewal and peace.

> **Sacred silence affirms the** *priority* **of sacred space and the first step in** *respect* **and honor to God in the wake of** *spiritual renewal* **and peace.**

Whatever is "worthy of praise" first requires stopping to think and consider Who or what it is you are praising. It demands a sense of quietness, quiet after an auspicious speech, the kind of quietness and humility you have while standing before a majestic mountain in its beauty. It requires awe like watching an orange sunset descending over the horizon against blue ocean waters. It requires a sense of wonder, child-like wonder like

---

16 Dionysius of Halicarnassus, *Roman Antiquities* IV.37.5.

17 Josephus, *Jewish Antiquities* 16:14; 17.200.

a child captivated by a flock of geese or a host of monarch butterflies in flight. If you lose child-like wonder you lose perspective, your life gets out of balance. Noise takes over, annoying, distracting, restless noise.

Next we look at the second step in sacred space, the importance of sacred speech. In the meantime, search for a sacred place to create sacred space, practice sacred silence, the stillness before God, and watch for doves, signs of peace. Begin the process of moving from noise, inner and outer noise, to quiet. *Be still and know that He is God. The Lord is in His holy temple; let all the earth be silent before Him* (Habakkuk 2:20).

Author's Note to the Reader

I just returned from the basketball court and swimming pool. Nothing refreshes me like perspiration from shooting hoops, swimming on a sunlit day, and cleaning house. The house is already clean, but I write creative lines after I clean house. My mother paid me to clean house as a boy. I like to clean the house.

When I returned from the pool, I thought this chapter lacked something. Not long ago I re-read Ernest Hemingway's book *The Torrents of Spring.* C. S. Lewis said somewhere that re-reading is a good practice. I practice it. As for Hemingway's book, I do not understand all the parts of it. Now *The Old Man and the Sea* I understand. A man and his boy wrestle a fish and the experience exhausts every ounce of energy. The sun beats down, the blue ocean churns, the boat rocks, the big fish pulls the line, leaps out of the water, and man's competitive edge does not wish for the fish to win.

Man must win, always. Does the old man battle the fish, the sea, or himself? Life burdens battle us like the heat of the sun. This demonstrates, at least to me, all the more reason why we need sacred space, sacred silence.

Hemingway in *The Torrents of Spring* entitled chapter two "The Struggle for Life." I only remember two sayings from the book: 1. "Literature has a strong effect on people's minds."[18] In the book Hemingway quotes the famed writer Henry Fielding, shares an anecdote about Henry James, and mentions Paris, which he always does in his books, because this paved the way for his literary

---

18 Ernest Hemingway, *The Torrents of Spring* (New York: Simon & Schuster Scrivner's Paperback Edition, 1996), 57.

fame. 2. Hemingway interfaces his characters and their struggle for life in the book a factory worker, a wife who leaves her husband, waitress at a restaurant, and Native American Indians in what he calls "the passing of a great race and the making and marring of American minds."[19]

Oh, the second thing I remember. I am getting to it. He wrote, "The warm wind blows. Inside the Indians strange longings were stirring. They knew what they wanted. Spring was coming at last was coming to the frozen little Northern town." Did *spring* foreshadow a better day, hope, renewal, a day when the flowers in life would bloom afresh?

I did not like Hemingway's book *The Torrents of Spring*. I wondered about Hemingway, his life, his personal torments and torrents, his lifestyle and his self-inflicted suicide. He once quipped about writing and said be sure to include the weather in novels. People like the weather: Spring rain dripping off the roof, sunshine in summer, golden leaves falling from trees in the gentle winds of a fall cold front, and the tickle of snowflakes on your nose in winter.

---

19 Hemingway, *The Torrents of Spring*, 71.

Speaking of weather, I write on July 4th, Independence Day. I am home alone. The family is scattered across USA: in the Kansas plains, the North Texas heat, and the mugginess of South Texas near the Gulf Coast. Today presents no fanfare or fireworks anticipated tonight. It presents an opportunity to write, periods of silence, and as you know, a trip to the pool.

I posted earlier today on my Facebook page: "America the beautiful. Home of the brave. God shed His grace on thee. There is no freedom without sacrifice. Thanks to all who sacrificed and still do sacrifice. And blessed is the nation whose God is the Lord...Psalm 33:12." I attached a picture of the American flag at the Texas Rangers baseball game while the National Anthem was sung. The flag covers the entire baseball field— red, white, and blue. I only received 34 "likes" on the post. America seemed busy in that moment. We pride ourselves, award metals to ourselves for being busy people. America is a busy place! But what about sacred space?

I will now follow Hemingway's advice. I live in Texas. Already heat beats down on the house. The temperature will be in the mid-nineties. My backyard fades green. Soon yellow will carpet my back yard as the sun dehydrates the earth as summer wanes. Deer eat the grapevine in my back yard in the cool, dew-drop mornings. Cool mornings fool you in Texas. Cool mornings alert you that heat soon arrives!

You did not know it, but I left for a minute or so and went into the garage. This time of year (remember, it is summer here in Texas?) I always check for snakes when I step into the garage. Two rattlesnakes took up residence in my garage in the last two summers. One appeared ribbon-like, a baby. Did you know a baby rattlesnake zaps more venom than an adult if it bites you? If you see a baby rattlesnake in the garage I suggest you be careful. You might even kill it. Beware, where baby lands momma can only be in watchful eye.

By the way, driving home from the pool earlier a car ran over a rattlesnake, long and winding, ugly, smashed, bleeding, flattened by tire treads in the sizzle of Texas heat frying the critter on black asphalt. Sometimes I drive to the park and play basketball and create sacred space. Sometimes I sit on the back porch in a white rocking chair and ponder life while the sun sets. I reflect, focus on Christ, and practice sacred space in sacred silence. It saves me. Refreshes me like swimming.

It renews me, gives my life balance. I wonder if Hemingway had practiced sacred space if it might have saved him. I wonder if someone close to him might have saved him had they practiced sacred space. Torrents tame in sacred space, calm, find Peace.

I need to tell you one more thing. By the way, I am standing as I write. I wear a swimsuit. It is almost dry. The swimsuit is Ralph Lauren with a red polo on the left leg. I also wear a black shirt with a red matching polo also on the left side of my body. To my left on the floor my black flip flops sit. I like my clothes to match. Do not make fun of me for this. Also to my left on the table I use an iPad to Google information and to check my facts like the one about Churchill writing while standing.

I reflect, *focus* **on Christ, and practice sacred space in** *sacred silence.* **It saves me.**

My feet hurt, but writing upright is good for my aching back. Besides, the famed orator, politician, and writer Winston Churchill preferred to take a wooden lectern, place it near a wall, and write while standing up. Churchill found peace by painting. He escaped into sacred space by taking a blank canvas and contrasting colors with a brush and paint. It calmed his nerves, worked new parts of his brain, and refreshed him. Watching a sunset while I pray to Jesus does that for me.

I still have not told you one more thing. Here it is. While driving home just after I saw the road-kill rattlesnake, I heard a song on the radio by Tim McGraw and Faith Hill. He will be surprised I discovered this nugget in his song, "Meanwhile Back at Mama's." I heard the song and wished I had traveled to see my parents on this July day. They created sacred space for me as a child by allowing me to roam the pond near the house of my youth while catching butterflies in a net and scooping up tadpoles from the pond and putting them in a Mason jar.

I loved the line in McGraw's song: "What I wouldn't give for a slow down, don't ya know? Cause where I come from, only the horse runs When the day is done, we take it easy." See, even Tim McGraw and Faith Hill long for space, the quiet of sacred space where sacred silence screams hope, joy, and peace. We long for a period of slow to gather our thoughts, to collect our nervous wits, and to take in the wonder of God's silence.

The song made me wish I was at my mama's and made me think of the green swing with a gentle breeze easing onto the porch and across my face. I have already told you about this sacred place, sacred space in my life. The North Carolina Mountains, any blue ocean, and any porch provide a good place to start with sacred space and the awe of sacred silence.

Author's Second Note to the Reader

Did you like this chapter? Will you practice sacred silence? Will you find a spot, a space to render sacred space a priority in your life? Trust me; it will make a huge difference in your life. I hope you really liked the chapter. Writers wonder about this, even worry about it. But as I have said, sacred space helps you handle worry.

Did you feel my pain when I talked about my church experience? Please do not fret over it. As I write I have a sense of peace in life and in God. Life, like a roller coaster, surprises us with twists and turns, ups and downs, mountains and valleys as I mentioned earlier. Have you forgotten already? Sacred silence centers your life and provides balance in your relationship with Christ.

I do, honestly, fear a corporate mindset, arrogance, and pride have crept into churches and power strong arms strangle the church. Sacred space invites us to Christ-like humility. Sacred silence slays arrogance and pride like a snake. "Humble yourselves, therefore, under God's mighty hand, that He may lift you up in due time. Cast your anxiety on Him because He cares for you," Saint Peter once wrote (I Peter 5:6-7). Sacred silence equips us with humility and creates space for us to place our cares at Jesus's feet.

Reader, did you feel lonely when I wrote about loneliness? Did you feel for me in being home alone with no fanfare and fireworks on the patriot's day, July 4th? Do you feel lonely now?

You might be lonely. In Cambridge, England several years ago I stayed at the SleeperZ, a hotel next to the train station. The noise of the crowd, the noise of the trains bouncing in and out of the station, and the weariness of my body taxed my soul. I checked into the hotel, slept off the weariness, and reclaimed my calm by sacred silence. I awoke the next morning, went down to breakfast on that crisp fall morning as the fog wisped across the green spaces in towering Cambridge and as the as the sun's rays fell through an open window. "Fresh" and "alive" described the morning.

Barry, a 60 year old man who worked at the hotel, offered me a croissant and orange juice. We talked and he spoke words I later wrote down. He uttered these words in soft tones, "C. S. Lewis once said that we read because we do not like the notion of being alone." Maybe you read because you do not like the notion of being alone. I could not find where Lewis said those exact words but I liked Barry's rendition. I write alone but, right now, I do not feel lonely. Loneliness, though, is something we can all feel at times. I have been there, too.

Did you identify with my sense of failure? Have you ever failed at something, dear reader, a job, school, an exam, a relationship, finances, or failed at a dream that died and left you feeling like you were in a fallen house burned to the ground and you were left in tears, hopeless, sitting in the ashes? Did you like it? Did you shed tears? Did you feel guilty? Did you want to quit on life? Did you scramble to find a counselor, a comforter?

Failure sends us on a tailspin. The roller coaster comes off the track. Sacred space and sacred silence remind us that failure might be the planted seed buried deep in the darkness of despair that emerges and grows into a colorful flower to both behold and smell in its scent of delight. Failure's night becomes a sacred moment to find

> **The torrents and** *struggles* **of life offer glimpses of hope if only we shed tears and seek Christ in** *sacred silence.*

grace and discover anew the light and wisdom of God's goodness. The torrents and struggles of life offer glimpses of hope if only we shed tears and seek Christ in sacred silence. By His strength you can rise from the ashes. He gives you a future and a hope (Jeremiah 29:11).

Reader, did it bother you that I mentioned Hemingway's suicide? After I wrote this chapter, actor Robin Williams took his life. *Time* magazine wrote, "So we recall Robin Williams as the stalwart friend whose generosity matched his genius, and the star who corralled his angels and demons and made the world laugh in the maddest, merriest way."[20]

---

20 Richard Corliss, "The Heart of Comedy," *Time* 184, no. 7 (August 25, 2014): 42-53.

My heart goes out to Hemingway's family and Williams's family. No one understands the pain of a family in the horrors of grief, even the guilt or misery that such a family lives through. Few understand grief's shadows. No one understands the pain, the misery, the angst, the anxiety, inner angels, much less demons, or the burdens, external and internal, that the average person carries.

While I know nothing of mental illness, self-inflicted pressure that explodes, or self-condemnation that leads to the destruction of self, I propose sacred space, the stillness before God, as a coping mechanism. A place to find mercy and help, a place to retrieve comfort, a place where you might discover the need of personal care or a community of care such as a professional counselor or church. A place that invites you to live with more compassion, empathy, and understanding for the people in the small circle of your world. After all, who knows the burden or the why of a burden that each person carries?

One compassionate person makes a difference. Sacred space makes a difference. Jesus in the *sacred space* makes a difference in you as you seek to live with compassion like Christ and empathy towards others. Pain often hides behind a mask and the sacred provides space to open your heart to God, self, and others.

Did your back stiffen and cringe when I talked about the rattlesnake? Did you want to protect the snake? Did you feel sorry for the snake? Did you even wonder as a curious person what kind of car ran over the snake, or, maybe, what kind of car I drive? After a sermon many years ago, a man reacted with anger when I talked about killing a snake. "You have prejudiced children and the whole congregation against snakes." The sermon came from Genesis and I wove a tapestry of words contrasting Adam and Eve in the Garden of Eden and the serpent's spell, his sinister ways.

The man felt strongly about snakes. People often possess strong opinions of snakes one way or another. I hope you do not miss the point in my writing like the man did in the snake sermon. I might have preached the woven words in a different way to be sure, but mine these gold nuggets in your life: Follow Christ. In life's struggle resist temptation. In sin, confess in the sacredness of a God who forgives. Anchor your life in God's power, His plan, His ways. Tether your life by creating sacred space. Calm your life by seeking Christ in routine sacred silence.

See there. You've almost finished this chapter. Maybe this chapter reads better now. Huh, reader? How many times did you check your phone, your Facebook, your computer, or your technology while you read this chapter? Has this chapter helped? Aren't we over-technologized and over-sensitized? Are you weary? Tired?

Tether your life by *creating* sacred space.

Try this: turn off your phone. Turn off all of your over-hyped technology. Sacred space offers quiet, a movement from noise, restlessness, annoyances like a spider dancing on your eardrum, to quiet. Be still, this is a sacred day (Nehemiah 8:11).

The Lord will fight for you, you need only to be still (Exodus 14:14). Be still before the Lord and do not fret when men succeed in their ways, when they carry out their wicked schemes (Psalm 37:7). Be still; refrain from anger and turn from wrath; do not fret, it only leads to evil (Psalm 37:8). Place your sword in the scabbard; cease and be still (Jeremiah 47:6). Be still before the Lord, all mankind, He has roused himself from his holy dwelling (Zechariah 2:13). "Quiet. Be still," Jesus said to the winds and waves in a storm to both calm the storm and His disciples (Mark 4:39). "Quiet. Be still," Jesus whispers to you, hushed and quiet in the echo of His still, small voice. Beware, though, Christ's whisper, His still small voice echoes, can even speak to your heart, mind, and soul in loud tones.

Now, close your eyes or sit on the back porch and watch the sun set. Listen to the silence. Listen for the sacred. Tune your ears to God's space, his mind, heart and soul. Do you hear it?

Okay reader, thanks for your patience. Now we proceed to sacred speech. Turn the page, reader. Thanks for reading. If you need a break, I understand. Step into the garage and sweep out the dust, the dead spiders, and the decayed brown leaves or find a porch swing. Be careful, though, if you enter your garage. It's summer. Watch for a rattlesnake. If you swing on the porch, I suggest you block out the chatter and noise of machines around you. Listen to the quiet.

Alert your ears to the music of birds singing. Listen closely. They like to sing "How Great Thou Art" with the words..."when I in awesome wonder consider all the worlds Thy hands have made." Some birds chirp, "Be still my soul." Maybe a few birds are singing, "Meanwhile back at mama's." Do you hear creation as it sings? Meanwhile, I move to the next chapter: Sacred Speech: from chaos to peace.

Sacred Speech
FROM CHAOS TO PEACE

*"I listen back to a time when nothing was much
further from my thoughts than God for an echo of
the gutterals and sibilants and vowelessness by
which I believe that even then God was addressing
me out of my life as He addresses us all. And it is
because I believe that, that I think of my life and of
the lives of everyone who has ever lived, or will live
ever live, as not just journeys through time but as
sacred journeys."*

~ Frederick Buechner, *The Sacred Journey*[21]~

---

21 Frederick Buechner, *The Sacred Journeys: A Memoir of
the Early Days* (New York: HarperCollins, 1982), 6.

When I went to the doctor to have my aching ear checked not long ago, the doctor looked in my ear. A doctor always checks the tongue on a routine visit. The depressor stick that looks like an over-sized Popsicle stick reveals much about the tongue and tonsils. While you gag, or try not to gag, the doctor analyzes your tongue. Did you know that your tongue operates as muscle in your body that serves as the organ of taste, a tool for eating food, and a key element in your speech? You might not want to know this or think of this but the tongue also helps keep your teeth clean.

The tongue functions in combination with skin, eight muscles, and taste buds known as papillae. A tongue averages about four inches in length and, occasionally, a person can touch the tip of his or her tongue to the tip of his or her nose. Such an act may seem like a circus trick or an amazing feat of individual ingenuity and prowess.

More amazing, though, are the taste buds, energizing and igniting nerves that run across your facial nerves and somehow stimulate other nerves that signal the brain. These signals that take the nerve train and enter your brain as good tastes, like maybe chocolate pie and spinach, or bad tastes like a bitter lime or lemon or juiced ginger devoured in apple juice. Tastes appear individual and preferential, and your tongue knows what tastes good to you and what tastes bad. The tongue knows what you like.

So far, I must say, I have attempted to simplify the tongue in its function. Actually, it is much more complex than this. I know you speak with your tongue, known as phonetics and phonology, to distinguish between the tip of the tongue and the part of the tongue behind the tip. What you know is that a baby says "dada" or "mama" for the first time and phonetics and phonology and maybe speech therapy (a father rehearsing for weeks...say "dad") are doing their glorious work. You also know that some words are easy to say like dog, cat, cow, is, and ice cream. And likewise some words are difficult to say like phonology, eschatology, tautological, disenfranchisement, preternatural, obstreperous, consubstantiation, orthicon, orchidaceous, ornithology, and orhnithological societies. Ornithological societies study birds, define their zoological category and their unique traits, the bluebird, redbird, cardinal, the hawk, the bald eagle, and the pint-sized humming bird.

A hummingbird could fit nicely on your tongue as it is about the same size. A hummingbird's heart beats about 1,263 beats a minute and flutters its wings in a figure eight motion in wonder at about 70 to 80 rotations per second when in flight. Say these interesting facts out loud and you discover an interesting phenomenon: whatever takes place in the floor of your mouth when the tongue activates its taste buds, nerves, and phonological aspects signal the brain.

> **Speech invokes** *promise,* **hope, and can wound like blade of a sword or** *cut deep* **like a knife.**

What results, in simple terms, is speech, language, verbal words declaring tastes (bitter!), happiness (a good day!), or facts (check the hummingbirds). It is no wonder that your first words as a child are known as your "mother tongue." Speech informs the world. Speech influences. Speech invokes promise, hope, and can wound like the blade of a sword or cut deep like a knife.

What interests me, though, are two things: the tongue's connection to the mind and speech as sheer force, an influential power that causes hurt, transforms thinking, and moves the crowd. Your brain, at its optimum, remembers, translates information, solves a problem in critical thinking, and filters nerve signals to encourage speech. The brain does much more than this you know, but apart from the brain no speech exits through the mouth by way of the tongue.

If you took your brain out and held it in your hand it would be slightly larger than the palm of your hand, weigh between three-four pounds, and would feel like a jelly-like substance. The brain at two percent of the human body consumes about 20 percent of the whole body's energy. Mental tiredness is a real possibility. It affects speech. Do not live under the illusion that a larger brain means you are more intelligent than someone with a smaller brain. The frazzle-haired Albert Einstein's brain weighed less than three pounds and his brain appeared smaller than the average.

In fact, stress on the brain and life in general appears at an all-time high—stress that affects relationships, work atmosphere, families, and daily transactions as common as making a phone call to your cell phone or television cable provider, and language in general, angry outburst, cursing, verbal assaults, and outrageous road rage. *Time* magazine reported earlier this year about the stressed out masses, the importance of being mindful, and stress reduction techniques. The article stated its thesis: "Finding peace in a stressed out, digitally dependent culture may just be a matter of thinking differently."[22] Kate Pickert shared informative research about reducing stress and techniques for coping, relaxing, and surviving stress in life.

Stress, the mind, and the tongue can combine to form a lethal combination: chaos. Never a day passes that I do not see and sometimes feel the stress-mind-tongue combination: a man yells at his child; a woman screams at her boss; a child shouts at his or her parents; a man who receives a traffic ticket curses the police officer; the frustration that creates embarrassment once shared publicly. "I did not mean to say that," a lady once said to me as her pastor after her verbal darts wounded my weary soul.

"It's okay," I replied, "But I think you did mean to say it. It's okay."

---

22 Kate Pickert, "The Art of Being Mindful," *Time* (February 3, 2014): 40-6. By quoting Pickert I am not advocating "Mind Based Stress Reduction," but simply highlighting the desperation people feel to find a resolve to reduce their stress.

I turned and walked off quickly after the brief exchange. Why did I let her off the hook? Why did I affirm her meanness? Why did I not seek to understand her wounds? Hurt people hurt people. This often happens when the stress-mind-tongue maneuver on overdrive.

A society that neglects the sacred is prone to stick its foot in its mouth. A person who refuses to take time for the sacred combined with over-loaded stress enhances the possibility of unsacred speech. Holiness pushed aside, mixed with high-octane, ambitious drive, a packed schedule, and the desire to dominate another or life itself, will eventually enact stress-mind-tongue ungodliness. An unholy mind begets ungodly speech. There is no way around it. The world yearns, cries out for sacred space that invites sacred speech.

Have you stopped to consider the chaos in the world? As I write war in Iraq and Syria propels chaos into the business, family trials, and military strategies of soldiers in battle. Drug cartels angle and peddle their abusive powers across the Texas borders. Yesterday in Pheonix, Arizona a huge, dark dust cloud, a wall of dust swept over the city enveloping the city, buildings, golf courses, homes, streets, and people in massive chaos. Somewhere in my files is the story of a surgeon who shares how parents are ruining their children by forcing them into sports, especially fathers who force their sons to pitch in baseball and ruin their arms from overthrowing only to require serious, season-ending and often career-ending arm surgery. Sports has created family stress, family chaos in many households.

High-powered political maneuvering in Washington and on Wall Street displays moments of frightening chaos for those involved. How much more can be said of faith, church, and world unrest instilling religious chaos? How much more can be said of families and friends attempting to survive amid chaos? How much more can be said of the ticking of the clock, the pressures of time, the constraints of time, and the sheer weariness of not enough time? Is it any wonder that we keep checking our clocks, looking at our watches, and obsessing over our cell phones in the pressures of not enough time?

I think of two stories. One story I remembered was of a lady who survived a horrific earthquake in California. The shaking cabinets and cups and plates and rattling windows and moving earth beneath her feet gave her pause to think of

Psalm 46:10, to look it up in the Bible, and to find rest and peace amid the chaos both during and after the quake. Psalm 46:10 reminds us of peace in the chaos by asking us to be still and know that God is God. Be still is an aspect of sacred silence that we have already talked about in chapter one.

The second story was of an Arkansas woman who made it to her birthday, number 116 to be exact. She cited key factors in her longevity, "Trusting in the Lord, hard work, and loving everybody."[23] I tried to think of all the chaos she has lived through: world wars, Hitler's march, the roaring fifties, the protests of the sixties and seventies, Vietnam, race riots,

Is it any wonder that we keep *checking* our clocks, looking at our watches, and *obsessing* over our cell phones in the *pressures* of not enough time?

segregation, desegregation, the Gulf War, endless middle east controversies, Y2K, September 11 and the fire fall of the twin towers in New York,

---

23   Jill Bleed, "116 Year Old Named Oldest Living American," *Dallas Morning News*, July 5, 2014, 5A.

the change of technology from black and white televisions in their fuzziness to HDTV, from the agricultural to industrial to informational, from party phone lines to cell phones where you can take pictures and check your e-mail, from the chaos of politics, social networks, and bank crises, to name a select few.

In the Jewish sense chaos was a void, a kind of emptiness. In the Greek sense chaos formed an abyss in the darkness, "the deep," infinite dark space, and a gap spiraling into the lower world. In the Roman sense chaos formed the world without order, a longing for an end to war where chaos stilled and peace rested over the land. The Roman poet Virgil longed for the Roman Emperor Augustus to end the chaos to institute order.

History records the Roman author, architect, and military engineer Vitruvius, writing his book on architecture, laying out an orderly way to build buildings, lay out cities, and the construction of things with Vitruvian virtues, known as the Vitruvian triad: solid, useful, and beautiful. According to the Latin biographer Suetonius, during the reign of the Roman Emperor Titus (A.D. 70-81) his domain experienced three catastrophic calamities of chaos: "...the eruption of Mount Vesuvius in

Campania, a fire at Rome which continued three days and as many nights, and a plague the like of which had hardly ever been known before."[24]

The chaos of the epidemic plague caused people to seek medicines, remedies, and sacrifices to end the plague. The chaos of the fire caused Titus to make a speech with simple words, "I am ruined," words that joined him and his people in grief as he instructed his army to rebuild the structures which had been lost. The eruption of the volcano Vesuvius on August 24, A.D. 79, so explosive that it breathed lava into the Bay of Naples, so sudden, destructive, and grievous due to the chaos it created, buried cities, houses, buildings, men, women, and children in the routine of their normal day. One buried city known as Pompeii has been excavated showing buildings, *insulae* (apartments), houses in their order, the marketplace, diaries, legal proceedings, pottery and the like, even people, covered, entombed, and somewhat preserved for archaeologists to study for posterity and research.

One might say out of the fire and lava, chaos ensued and relics and people were frozen in time. As laws declared legal proceedings and

---

24 Suetonius, *The Deified Titus* 8.3-4.

bowls prepared for meals sat on tables, faces frozen in fear and people running for their lives were frozen in time like a fly in amber, solidified for archeologists to dissect and study years later like petrified wood in a forest. The chaos struck like lightening, paralyzed its victims, and revealed a lesson for the generations to follow: time proves precious; value time; take time.

> **Sacred speech is an** *invitation* **to enter into sacred space, to block out time, and to** *talk to Christ...*

It also serves a lesson for the present in your life: recreate for sacred space and practice sacred speech. The chaos of a 21st century world with its own firestorms, windstorms, and sand storms, albeit personal storms, no doubt, creates all kinds of panicked speech. You might even add gossip, bitter speech, angry, hate-filled speech, words in frustration, and speech like arrows hurled to hurt. Add sickness like an unwelcome plague of disease, a moment of fierce unexpected destruction like a swift fire, or an unplanned horror like a volcano spewing lava into the order of your neat and planned-out life, and you have the recipe for chaotic speech and chaos in its absence of peace.

Sacred speech is an invitation to enter into sacred space, to block out time, and to talk to Christ in preparation for living life to its fullest, for squeezing the most out of your time, and in placing value on the present moment. Notwithstanding, sacred speech also prepares you, ahead of time, for dealing with the inevitable catastrophes, calamities, and chaotic moments that will both interrupt and bless your life.

What is sacred speech? Sacred speech like one coin with two sides includes, first, God's Word speaking to you, and second, you speaking to God. I mentioned the Greek and Roman world, because like our world today, people often seek solutions for their catastrophes, calamities, and chaos. The Greeks and Romans did the same, trying anything from ritual prayers, to acts of worship involving sacrifice at pagan temples, to sorcery, asceticism, and even charitable indulgences in hopes of receiving benefits and favor from the ancient gods.

I could almost remove "Greek and Romans," and substitute "Americans" or "Germans" or "Great Britains" or "Koreans" or "Columbians" or "Texans," for that matter. It seems, all round the world in neighborhoods where you live, and in human hearts, a cry for peace, an incessant shout for an end to the chaos, reverberates throughout. The chaos swirls. The cry for an end to chaos deafens.

Sacred speech is informed by God-speech, God speaking through His Word. I cannot say enough about reading the Scriptures on a daily basis. Read Genesis to see how God makes order out of chaos, transforms by wrestling with God the non-spiritual into the spiritual (Jacob), and redeems evil and produces good, not only for the harmed, but also for others (Joseph).

Read the Torah, the first five books in the Bible, to discover God's plan for you, order in the sense of holiness, living under the umbrella of His goodness, and His work of forgiveness. Read the historical books to the Bible to discover how order and chaos, good and evil, intertwine, collide, and sometimes co-exist, but how God desires order, His good, and how He overpowers chaos and evil to reveal Himself as a God of righteousness, peace, and joy.

Read the Psalms and Old Testament books of poetry to find balance in the chaos of your life. Especially read the Psalms as, according to the German theologian and martyr Dietrich

Bonhoeffer, "It is grace to know God's commands" (Word).[25] He also adds, "God's speech in Jesus Christ meets us in the Holy Scriptures."[26] God's Word, the Psalmist affirms, reminds us of God's grace, goodness, and glory as it breaks into our personal chaos to order and deliver peace to our hectic lives.

The Psalmist also warns. C. S. Lewis notes, "Against all this the ferocious (warnings of evil) parts of the Psalms serve as a reminder that there is in the world such a thing as wickedness and that it (if not its perpetrators) is hateful to God."[27] The Psalms admonish sacred space as a necessary ingredient to nurture the soul so that a pure heart, mind, and tongue result. Sacred speech via the Word encourages sacred speech via the tongue. More will be said about this later in the chapter.

Read the poets and prophets of the Word. The poets as prophets mean that they chose their words carefully. Their words, crafted and wielded

---

25   Dietrich Bonhoeffer, *Psalms: The Prayer Book of the Bible* (Minneapolis, Minnesota: Augsburg, 1974), 31.

26   Bonhoeffer, *Psalms: The Prayer Book*, 11. He also notes: "If we wish to pray with confidence and gladness, then the words of Holy Scripture will have to be the solid basis of our prayer" (11-12).

27   C. S. Lewis, *Reflections on the Psalms* (Orlando, Florida: Harcourt and Brace, 1956), 33.

like a sword, piercing the ears and heart like rolling thunder, speak to the core of sacred speech
God's Word active, sharp, piercing both the bone
and marrow, discerning the thoughts and intents
of the wise and the foolish (Hebrews 4:12).

The prophet as poet borrows from society,
daily life, and nature to communicate God's truth
in such a way as to arrest the senses, awaken the
heart. The poet wrestles with God, life, and words,
and translates it into sacred speech by the Holy
Spirit as a means of plowing your heart. Reading
the prophet as poet produces a Divine encounter,
sacred silence and sacred speech combining to
enrich the soul and startle the senses to fresh vision.

The prophets as poets might fall in line
with a devotional poet like George Herbert (1593-
1633). His poetry possessed "an energy, inven-
tiveness and intellectual depth and edge" that
combined brain-work, heart-work, and heaven-
work to instill in the reader a sense that the poet
as prophet is "pleading with God or arguing with
him, or disputing with himself, but always talking
to other men."[28] So Jeremiah prophetically asked

28　D. J. Enright, ed., *George Herbert: Everyman's Poetry*
(London: Guernsey Press, 1996), xiv-xv.

God, "Why does the way of the wicked prosper?" (Jeremiah 12:1). Isaiah pleads, "God, have you not known, nor heard that the Everlasting God, the Creator of the universe does not grow tired and weary and that He gives strength to the tired, weary, and weak?" (Isaiah 40:28-31).

The poet-prophet and fig-picker from Tekoa, Amos, lashed out to a non-repentant society, "Seek me and live. Seek the Lord and live. Seek good and not evil that all may be well with you" (Amos 5:4, 6, 14). Amos may have spoken for all prophets when he uses wide-eyed images of locust, plumb lines, fire, and summer fruit to declare God's judgment, but also his promise of restoration, healing the broken places, and renewal in the land of new vineyards, fresh wine, and fruitful gardens. The prophets as poet remind us as surely as the garden fails that God can bring fresh rain, new seeds, and new days when the crop bears fruit to revive the soul.

Read the prophets as poets to awaken the soul, but read them as thunderbolts with prophetic words in a call to new action in your life. The prophets "throw light upon our own day and our won situation by announcing the eternal principles of divine providence which will always operate whenever similar conditions are present."[29] Isaiah calls for new light (Isaiah 9:2). Jeremiah laments, but cries for an end to grief, a resurrection of compassion, a faithful transfer of God's love and compassion as new for every morning, as fresh as dew on the morning grass (Lamentations 3:22).

Ezekiel declares hope, a time when hearts of stone melt into soft hearts, a new spirit of love, knowledge, and obedience to Christ, a wonderful day when dry bones spring to life and hope tingles (Ezekiel 36-37). Daniel alludes to new freedom, albeit from lion's dens to courageous acts of service to the King (Daniel 10:18). Hosea allowed God a refuge (Joel 3:16). The forsaken, melancholy, bruised and broken Hosea plowed the hard ground of repentance that leads to return, forgiveness, and healing in the hands of God who renews the heart like dew, who turns from anger, and who forgives sin while instilling the sweet scent of life like an evergreen tree (Hosea 14). Micah called for the same (Micah 7:18), "Who is a God like you who pardons and forgives?"

---

29 Kyle M. Yates, *Preaching from the Prophets* Nashville, Tennesssee: Broadman Press, 1942), 1.

Nahum promises good news (Nahum 1:15). Habakkuk admonishes a day of rejoicing that will cause us to jump like a deer (Habakkuk 3:1-19). Zephaniah, Haggai, Zechariah, and Malachi hail God's presence, his power, and his providence as reigning King in your life and as a son whose righteousness rises like the sun "with healing in its wings" (Malachi 4:2). The prophets when read and heard as God's sacred speech tilt your heart toward a new start, a new day, and new resolutions that enliven a new spirit.

> **The prophets when** *read and heard* **as God's sacred speech tilt your heart toward a new start, a new day, and new resolutions that** *enliven* **a new spirit.**

Read the New Testament: the four Gospels as they unfold the drama, life, and transforming work of Christ as Gospel, good news as enthralling and inviting as any good news in your own life. Read the letters of the apostle Paul, how in his travels, church planting, and life experience, he discovered the joy of Christian discipline like a soldier, athlete, and farmer, except the stakes were much higher (2 Timothy 2).

One cannot read Paul's letters without thinking of his bi-vocational ministry of tent-making, of his encounters with Roman oppression, of his fettered days in jail, and his endless spirit of righteousness, joy, and peace in the Holy Spirit (Romans 14:17). And who can read Paul's letters without thinking of the pettiness between people, the back-stabbing, church fights, and trivial squabbles of what to eat or drink or where to sit when table fellowship and unity seemed so much more important than petty, selfish, stone-hearted opinions that diminished the light of Christ.

Paul, ever so pastoral, ever so glued to the sacred, ever so insightful on the human condition because of the gravity of his own sin and the humility of Christ, ever so hopeful of human transformation, seemed nearly always to come down on the soft side of grace and on the gentle wind of wisdom in his words as his sacred speech uttered words of reconciliation and forgiveness. He always clamored for change, Christ-change in the souls gone amiss, exploding with words of reform, revolution, and innovation.

Be transformed by the renewing of your mind! Put on the Lord Jesus Christ! Do not become weary in doing good! Bear one another's burdens! Rejoice in the Lord! Be strong in the grace that is in Christ Jesus! Devote yourself to doing what is good! And remember, nothing can separate us from the love of Christ, not death, life, demons, the present or the future, nor unseen powers, not height nor depth, not any other creature (Romans 8:38-39)!

Read Paul because he knew the challenges of the Christian life as well as the hopes, dreams, joys, and blessings overflowing like a river brimming the edges and filtering into farmer's fields to provide fresh water for the coming harvest. Take Paul's advice, "Follow my example as I follow the example of Christ (I Corinthians 11:1). Paul uses the word *mimetas*, "mime" or "mimic," a word indicating his desire to copy Christ, to act like Christ, to imitate Christ in thought, action, conduct, service, and speech. Paul's letters draw a picture of what it means to imitate Christ, to mimic sacred speech.

Read Hebrews that instigates faith in Christ as the operative source of running, enduring, and finishing life's race (Hebrews 12). Read the Book of James never forgetting that James the half-brother of Jesus wrote as a brother, pastor, and fellow-struggler on the journey of faith in its richness and, oftentimes, its prickliness. Read James for inspiration and for instruction on what it means to face trials, be a friend of God, treat people according to the golden rule (James sounds so much like Jesus), and to understand patience in trials, humility in a world of pride, and patience in a runaway world where sacred speech often falls on deaf ears.

Read Peter's epistles, bold and brash as he was. Read John's, the beloved epistles bubbling with love that so characterized his life. Read Jude as apocalypse and prophetic thunder like one of the Old Testament prophets. Read the Revelation for what it is, God's "unveiling," His revelation of Himself to you in a book of worship for tough times, trying times, uncertain times, and end times. Read the Revelation to discover that God gets the last Word and that God still speaks victory into apparent defeat, rivers of life into wilderness dust, and grand, glorious, good news like a birth announcement (Jesus is coming!) that overshadows and overpowers all the bad news heard on the nightly news.

Read the Bible as sacred scripture, God's sacred speech written to you and held together by a single thread. Frederick Buechner applauds scripture as "...held together by having one single plot. It is one that can be simply stated: God creates the world, the world gets lost; God seeks to restore the world to the glory for which He created it."[30] Read the scripture as sacred speech to experience renewal, restoration, even salvation and the glory of a new day with a new outlook and a new destination (heaven) in new clothes. Put on Jesus Christ. Dress up for life as simply as you dress for your day.

> **Read the Bible as *sacred* scripture, God's sacred speech written to you and *held together* by a single thread.**

God's sacred speech as His Word, as His word to you, and as sacred scripture which He longs to plant like seed in your heart, creates and re-creates sacred speech, that is, a tongue and speech that please Christ. Apart from sacred speech, the Word God speaks and has spoken

---

30 Frederick Buechner, *Secrets in the Dark: A Life in Sermons* (New York, NY: HarperCollins, 2006), 194.

through His Word and Jesus, there is no *sacred* speech.

The other day it occurred to me that so much is said in the Bible about the tongue because the tongue has so much potential to get it wrong. It also crossed my mind that so much chaos and clutter in the world stems from chaotic hearts that breed un-sacred speech such as harsh words, mean words, caustic speech, critical speech, and coarse speech in the form of dirty words, cursing, and anger lashed out. Chaos spurns chaotic speech. Un-sacred hearts vomit speech lacking the sacred. Sacred hearts rejuvenate sacred speech.

At the outset we said that sacred speech is like two sides to a coin: God speaking to you; you speaking to God. I like to intertwine one coin with two sides: to read (the Bible) and talk to God (pray!); to pray and read God's sacred speech. Do this simultaneously: Read. Stop. Pray. Talk to God. Read. Stop in silence. Pray out loud and talk to God like you talk to a friend on your cell phone or over a conversation at dinner.

How can you develop your sacred speech as prayer? Frank Moyle says, "Prayer is the elevation of the mind to God." Prayer focuses on Christ, His still small voice, and climaxes in "an offering of one's whole self, thus *inspired* or renewed, in an act of speech which consequently comes to have more of God in it than of oneself."[31] Too much of prayer highlights the self, your wants, your needs, your dreams and your desires rather than aiming toward Christ in His power, plan, and purpose of righteousness, joy, and peace. One aspect of prayer, Moyle informs, includes "the inner response of the human soul toward God."[32] Such a response in prayer moves the soul from chaos toward peace. It supplies tranquility. It fills the air with stillness. It soothes. It comforts. Christ calms the storm. He also calms the soul fighting the chaos of the storm.

Prayer follows many forms if you read Philippians 4:6, "Be anxious for nothing but by prayer and supplication, with thanksgiving, let your requests be made known to God." A combination of these prayer forms moves you out of chaos and into God's all-surpassing peace.

First, do not be anxious. This indicates a burden, a care that weighs you down or oppresses the mind and heart because it causes you to obsess on its negative aspects. Do we not live in

---

31 Frank W. Moyle, *The Book of Uncommon Prayer* (London: Andrew Dakers, 1949), 27.

32 Moyle, *The Book of Uncommon Prayer*, 27.

the age of anxiety where worry over terror, family, fiances, politics, the economy, jobs, stress, and the inevitable worry about *worry*? Prayer is *not* worry.

David Ulnin notes that we live in age of "hyperconnectivity" where endless streams of texts, news, and information overload brain circuits and cause us to "face endless anxiety about our ability to keep up, to maintain a place amid the onslaught, to make sense of all the data and what it means."[33] The age of anxiety and overload all the more necessitates sacred space and sacred speech.

> **The age of anxiety and** *overload* **all the more** *necessitates* **sacred space and sacred speech.**

Stop being anxious. Stop the worry is the first step in prayer. Calm the mind. Settle in Christ's peace.

A second step in prayer Paul designates as *proseuche*, a prayer of general devotion. I would

33 David L. Ulin, *The Lost Art of Reading: Why Books Matter in a Distracted Time* (Seattle: Sasquatch Books, 2010), 77.

call this your "Hello God" prayer over morning coffee, on the drive to work, or at your desk before you start your day.

This prayer reverberates Psalm 118:24, "This is the day the Lord has made, let us rejoice and be glad in it." *Proseuche* indicates sacred space for sacred speech. A *proseuche*, according to the soldier, statesman, prophet, Pharisee, Jewish priest, and historian Flavius Josephus (A.D. 237-97), was a designated place of prayer often built outside the city near a river or the sea when there was no synagogue in the city.[34] Roman laws actually protected such places as sacred space. Think of it as a prayer garden. A woman, Lydia, prayed near the river in Philippi in such a place and came to Christ there.

General daily devotion in prayer may be your most difficult challenge in prayer as sacred space. Maintaining discipline in prayer, or a diet or exercise or on the job or at school often proves taxing to even the most devoted. We live in an age of anxiety, yes. We also live in an age of distraction where the rewired brain and overtaxed eyes-minds appear to overwork "coding and

---

34 Josephus, *Jewish Antiquities* 14.258.

decoding."[35] Fewer books are read, yet the equivalent of a small book is being read daily by the average person when you consider texts, news feeds, the Internet, and office e-mail. People read more and digest less. People read tall stacks of information, but develop smaller minds because less depth of reading, and praying for that matter, takes place. Sacred speech encourages reading, praying, a time, a place, and prayer covered under the umbrella of scripture.

A third step of prayer is *requests*. Think of this as your prayer list. You read the Scripture and pause and pray over your list. Your prayer list involves all the people, things, events, and stuff that you might worry about from the family to finances to a stronger faith in the chaos and travail.

A fourth prayer is *thanksgiving*. The word thanksgiving in Greek is akin to the eucharist, the Lord's Supper, meaning that the death, burial, and resurrection of Christ is a good place to start and that all other gratitude, blessings, and appreciative words to God flow from the prior events of Christ's life. Where would we be without Christ? Where would you be? Yes, thank God for an air

---

35 Alan Jacobs, *The Pleasures of Reading in the Age of Distraction* (Oxford: University Press, 2011), 31.

conditioner in a hot Texas summer, for a car that takes you to work, for your vocation and vacation, for your in-laws, and for your daily breath, but precede it all with thanks to God for His indescribable gift of Jesus!

A fifth prayer step is another type of request, but I like to imagine it as a transaction of trust. The word indicates in its original form in Geek a financial transaction. In Greek and Roman society such a financial transaction filtered under obligations and benefits. This kind of prayer involves a pledge to trust God and to trust that He knows best, that His chosen benefits and answers to prayer benefit you and His kingdom the best.

In this prayer I like to call upon the Lord because of His greatness, goodness, and grace (Jeremiah 33:3). In this prayer you, in the words of the Psalmist, pour out your heart to God. He can handle your words, however, whenever, whatever. "Trust in Him at all times; you people, pour out your heart before Him; God is a refuge for us" (Psalm 62:8). A refuge protects, provides, and delivers peace.

Prayer as sacred speech inclines us to trust God and rest in His peace. We discover that we can cast our burdens on Him because He sustains us (Psalm 55:12). We accept His mercy as a gift. "I trust in the mercy of God forever and ever" (Psalm 53:8). Finally, we know He hears us as well as cares for us. "Evening, and morning, and at noon, will I pray, and cry aloud; and He shall hear my voice" (Psalm 55:17). Sacred speech links your heart to God's voice, and, in a sense, your voice to God's heart. Who could ask for anything more?

Author's Note to the Reader

Eh, reader, how did you like this chapter? Sacred speech includes God's Word, God talking to you and the other side of the coin, you talking to God. That seems simple enough, huh?

I wondered when I wrote about the tongue at the beginning of the chapter when I mentioned the doctor's visit and tongue depressor if you gagged. Did you think of your own tongue? Did thoughts of your own tongue feel gross? Did you think of your own tongue and words that were spoken with venom? Did you know that a blue speckled poison dart frog lives in the Amazon in Central and South America in tropical rainforests and its tongue produces toxic poison? The Native American Indians placed the toxic substance on the tips of their arrows to assist in killing their prey.

Did you know that James says the tongue can be full of deadly poison, that the tongue should not serve as a tool to curse but to bless, that a tongue that spews bitter speech displeases God, and that the tongue both poisons and destroys like a destructive forest fire (James 3)? Beware to use your speech to bless God and bless others. Sacred speech helps.

What did you think about Einstein's small brain? When I write I sometimes devour blueberries. One of my daughters once texted me five benefits of blueberries: cancer fighters; good for your bladder; reduce inflammation; promote healthy digestion; and increase your brainpower. The blueberries, I hope, fire my brain and increase my brainpower, but this chapter focuses on the heart, a heart open to God's Word that fixates in the heart, soul, and brain so as to promote healthy speech. Eat

> **Beware to use your speech to *bless* God and bless others. Sacred speech *helps*.**

blueberries. Delight in a healthy lifestyle. Long for healthy speech that delights God and people.

What about chaos? Did you identify with chaos in your own life? I find so much chaos surrounds people and causes a loss of alertness to life and surroundings. At the pool the other day I noticed a mother oblivious to her child who talked to her because of technological chaos, checking her e-mail. Another man told me about his own son, so embroiled in political chaos that he constantly checks his phone and neglects his family.

While I wrote this chapter you will not believe what happened. Associated Press reported the story of a 66 year-old woman in Chesire, Connecticut who was found dead in her home after her second floor caved in on her. Neighbors described her as a hoarder, but the chaos of her home became a death trap, literally.

I felt compassion for the woman's family, wondered if it might have been prevented, and felt a sense that, possibly, chaos caves in on the living as much as the dead, killing the soul as much as the body. Sacred speech supplies life to the soul and encourages sacred speech that spreads the good news of Christ and the antidote to poisonous speech: love.

Speaking of good news, I must tell you something. Reader, did you notice that I wrote the words "good news" five times already in this chapter and that good news is sure hard to keep under wraps?

Subconsciously, this good news keeps flowing out of my blueberry brain. I have a secret. I am not supposed to share this, but by the time you read this the news will run wild like berries on a vine. My oldest daughter and her husband will have a baby. My middle daughter and her husband will also have a baby. Are you excited? I will be a grandfather, "Grandpa Doc" as they dubbed me. When they told me the news I almost cried. Yes! Yes! Yes!

Did you remember that I wrote these words: "...God gets the last Word and that God still speaks victory into apparent defeat, rivers of life into wilderness dust, and grand, glorious, good news like a birth announcement (Jesus is coming!) that overshadows and overpowers all the bad news heard on the nightly news!" Good news travels like a birth announcement. Sacred speech generates glorious speech more exciting than a new birth. Yes! Yes! Yes! So much for those words, the backstory printed in black ink. Use your blueberry brain to shout glorious good news in Christ to rid the blues!

Reader, do you like good news? If you allow God to speak to you through His Word and if you talk to Him in prayer, chances are, I am sure, that your speech will sprinkle salt and shine light. Did not Jesus say that Christians should salt, preserve, and spice up the world? And Jesus said that Christians ought to uncover their light, not hide it under a bushel, and let their melodious, joyous voices be lifted high to radiate the light of Christ. Sprinkle salt with speech. Shine light as sacred speech.

> **Sacred speech** *generates* **glorious speech more** *exciting* **than a new birth.**

Three things happened while I finished this chapter. First, another person and I had some miscommunication. While we handled it well, sacred speech did not flow easily, but sacred speech resolved the miscommunication. Sacred speech heals, forgives, and reconciles.

I do not want you to think that sacred speech is as easy as pie. Miscommunication happens and might free-flow unsacred speech. Hurt people hurt people and harsh words might be part of the dynamite. Somewhere I read not long ago where *100 million* Americans live with chronic pain. Physical pain might yield unsacred speech. An argument with your spouse, a bad day at work, children out of control, road rage, anger at your friend who betrayed you, and chaos building like a volcano might explode with fire, white hot, flowing verbal lava, and ashes that settle and harden.

By the way, did you like the reference to Vitruvius, the Roman architect, and to Vesuvius, the volcano at Pompeii in A.D. 79? Do not confuse Vitruvius and Vesuvius. It seemed to me to describe the day and age in which we live, boiling frustration beneath the surface and fire flashed, spewing words above the surface. It seemed to me to accentuate the need for slowing down, stopping in sacred space, and inviting sacred speech into your life. Will you try sacred speech and commit to it? It requires discipline, daily routine and regular discipline that requires you to put down your technology, to lift up your heart and soul to Christ, and to bend down in humility as God speaks.

A second thing happened as I wrote this chapter. I took out the trash twice. I am good at taking out the trash. Today when I took the trash out to the garbage can I saw a bird in flight, the green leaves on my oak trees blowing in the wind, and rain clouds. Later, it rained; showers here in Texas on a hot July day. Summer showers provided a welcome sight in the draining Texas heat that refreshed the parched earth. I think I heard the grass singing, "Hallelujah!"

I watched the dark storm clouds, zeroed in with my eyes on the distant, pouring rain dropping from the heavens in curved lines as it fell, and hoped for prophetic thunder and lightning that never came. Remember in the last chapter, Ernest Hemingway reminded me to be sure and tell you about the weather? Everyone finds interest in the weather. It rained. Rain refreshed the earth. Should I say it? You know by now I would say this kind of thing, huh, reader: sacred speech refreshes heaven and earth? Beware, I am coming back to Hemingway in a moment. I like Hemingway.

When I took out the trash, forgive me for this bizarre insight, but I thought of "dung." I preach the Good News on Sundays and find myself reflecting on words like "dung." The apostle Paul speaks a sacred, holy word, "Yea doubtless, and I count all things but loss for the excellency of the knowledge of Christ Jesus my Lord: for whom I have suffered the loss of all things, and do count them but dung, that I may win Christ, and be found in him..." (Philippians 3:8).

Did you see the word dung there? Dung is *skubala* in Greek that which is thrown to the dogs, refuse, trash, and, in its most industrious use, fertilizer spread and smeared over dirt to nourish the farmer's field. The prominent Roman naval commander, equestrian, and writer Pliny the Elder (A.D. 23-A.D. 79), who died while attempting to rescue a friend at the hands of the monster volcano Mount Vesuvius, wrote in *Natural History*, "Strains and bruises are treated with dung, wild boar's dung gathered in spring and dried. This treatment is used for those who have been dragged by a chariot or mangled by its wheels or bruised in any way. Fresh dung may also be smeared on" (Pliny, *Natural History* 28.237).[36]

"Dung" appears sick, smells like stink, and must be cast aside, taken out like trash. For sacred space to transform your life you must, there is no shortcut or attempt to navigate around it, you must clear the chaos for a brief time, remove

---

36 Pliny the Elder, as quoted by J. C. Mckeown, *A Cabinet of Curiosities: Strange Tales and Surprising Facts from the World's Greatest Empire* (Oxford: University Press, 2010), 73.

the clutter in your life, and clear out the trash that stacks up and keeps you from the freedom that sacred speech aims to provide. Sacred speech demands destruction of the "dung," but it also requires taking the hard things in life, even harsh words spoken to you, and the difficult things as fertilizer, soul nutrients for future growth, and as dung smeared on wounds to heal. That seems sick, gross doesn't it? But it works like fertilizer in the heart as dung is to a farmer's dirt for nurturing his crop.

Paul counted *all* things loss for the sake of Christ, a sacred act of clearing sacred space for God to work in your life. He also weighed and counted such things as dung, fertilizer, and a balm for healing wounds deep in the heart that he might win Christ. Paul's virtue rested in Christ.

His goal to follow Christ and serve him (Philippians 2:5-11) motivated him toward a sense of the sacred. Paul had to put the past behind him and press toward a higher goal of God's upward call (Philippians 3:12-14). This higher call in his life and yours, mind you, calls for a vision for God's higher call that inspires sacred speech as a daily routine and a way of life.

Do you realize how challenging sacred speech can be? How you might be tempted to lash out at people verbally, to spit hate-filled speech, to shout angry words, and to let bitterness boil and explode into poisonous words like darts from a poisonous arrow? Do you understand how easy it is to criticize? Remember in chapter one when I told you about what happened at church? Should I confess that for a season I fought the strong temptation to surrender to caustic speech, bitter words, and angry thoughts that might have spilled over into vengeful words of revenge? Should I tell you I love the church, that church, and other churches more than ever before? I do. I really do.

Do you realize how *challenging* **sacred speech can be?**

Should I tell you that God's Word, His sacred speech convicted me, challenged me, and comforted me in my wounds? Should I tell you that I cast much of it aside as dung, trash carried out in an effort to clear the chaos, clutter, and cast-off pride necessary for me to focus on God's future for my life? Should I tell you that I had to smear the dung, dry it out, and spread it around in the soil of my soul so as to nurture and prepare my soul to minister in God's future and hope that He has for me (Jeremiah 29:11)? Should I tell you that dung stinks, that sometimes life stinks, but that sacred speech nourishes the soul for sacred speech, words that praise God, encourage the saints, and build up the body of Christ? Should I repeat myself: *this is not easy*, nor was it meant to be.

Surely, you have not forgotten, have you? Hurt people hurt people. The criticized reflexively lean toward criticizing others. The wounded naturally aim to hurt others. The dunged prefer not to smear the dung in their hearts, but to dump dung on others. Sacred speech eliminates dung, recycles it for future use, and anticipates its enrichment in the soil of the soul as fruitful speech and healing, comforting words.

I told you I would return to Hemingway. He hated his critics. He said, "Criticism is dung anyway. Nobody knows anything about it (your book) except yourself. God knows people who are paid to have attitudes toward things, professional critics, make me sick..."[37] Hemingway said interesting

---

37 Larry W. Phillips, ed., *Ernest Hemingway on Writing* (New York, New York: Scribner, 1984), 138.

things like, "You must be prepared to work [write] without applause."[38]

Likewise, sacred space and sacred speech plea for time alone with no applause. Hemingway also said sometimes he picked up one of his books and said, "Why this stuff is bloody marvelous."[39] Hemingway had confidence in his writing, quite frankly, that I do not have. Hemingway might have bordered on arrogant, puffed with pride, over-zealous in his charge to literary masterpieces. Sacred speech ought to have the opposite effect, not boastful arrogance, but humility; not puffed up pride, but a spirit of grace; not overzealous ambition, but humble service. Sacred speech causes you to acknowledge God's goodness, His wonder and causes you to marvel at His grace and humility.

Oh, did you see that in old Hemingway? It was subtle. You might have missed it. He hated his critics and, in turn, lashed out at his critics. Unsacred criticism and speech proves a vicious cycle of lament, woe, and poison arrows aimed to hurt. It spins a vicious cycle and an unending circle that is

---

38   Phillips, ed., *Ernest Hemingway on Writing*, 139.

39   Phillips, ed., *Ernest Hemingway on Writing*, 140.

seldom broken unless you practice sacred speech. Are you in yet? On sacred speech? *All* in?

Writers help us here. Fiction writer Stephen King notes, "The biggest aid to regular production [in writing] is a serene atmosphere."[40]

Unsacred **criticism and speech proves a vicious cycle of lament, woe, and poison arrows** *aimed to hurt.*

The old man Hemingway said, "To have come on all this new world of writing, with time to read in a city like Paris... was like having a great treasure given to you."[41] The Canadian fiction writer Margaret Atwood of the eclectic book on writing, *Negotiating with the Dead*, describes her experience of discovering that she wanted to be a writer as captivating, exciting, saying, "It was the electricity."

Substitute *sacred speech* for writing and you have the joy of sacred speech: necessary, although short-lived serenity in the chaos; sacred speech as a delightful treasure both enjoyed and

---

40   Stephen King, *On Writing: A Memoir of the Craft* (New York, New York: Scribner, 2000), 154.

41   Phillips, ed., *Ernest Hemingway on Writing*, 102.

cherished; and "the electricity," God, Jesus, and the Holy Spirit delivering Peace.

Do not forget that sacred space moves from chaos to peace, from a whirlwind to the calm wind of the Holy Spirit that blows on, in, and through you. Peace passes all understanding, guards your heart and helps you use your tongue to build up, not tear down, to lift up, not throw under (the bus), and to draw others into God's high calling. I think that sums up this chapter? Is it sinking in?

P.S. – To the Reader

Reading over this chapter makes me think I left something out. This happens to writers and the reader goes, did he leave something out? I mentioned the three things that happened. I told you of two: the miscommunication and the fact that I am good at taking out the trash, dung and all that. What was the third thing? I just remembered. While I was writing this chapter, 1936 Olympic athlete and WWII military hero Louis Zamperini died in Los Angeles at ninety-seven years of age.

Lauren Hillenbrand, herself a remarkable story as she wrote the book in the throes of chronic fatigue syndrome, wrote the best-selling book about Zamperini: *Unbroken: A World War II Story of Survival, Resilience, and Redemption.* The book title details in summary LZ's life: a pilot shot down in the Pacific, survived on a raft for 45 days while avoiding sharks, was captured, tortured, freed, and later experienced the life of Christ and became a Christian.

The story is dramatic, life-changing, and too long for my purposes here, but two simple, yet sacred things stand out: First, sacred speech moved, initially, LZ's heart toward Christ while he starved in prison and endured horrific torture when he prayed to the Lord, "If you will save me, I will serve you forever."[42] God slipped His hand down and rescued LZ by miracles, wondrously and mysteriously.

Second, sacred speech influenced his new heart as he followed Christ so much that he aimed to meet, reconcile, and forgive his persecutors. He wrote a letter to one torturer stating, "Love replaced the hate I had for you. Christ said, *Father forgive your enemies and pray for them.*"[43] Sacred

---

42   Laura Hillenbrand, *Unbroken:A World War II Story of Survival, Resilience, and Redemption* (New York: Random House, 2010), 375.

43   Hillenbrand, *Unbroken*, 397.

speech linked to Christ sets the soul free to forgive and fills the heart with love.

This is good news? Do you like the good news? I am excited about being a grandfather soon. My daughters are excited, too. The whole family is bouncing-off-the-wall excited! What good news!

Another piece of good news comes. Thanks to my middle daughter who bought the book by clergyman Frank W. Moyle *The Book of Uncommon Prayer*. I got stuck on this chapter, the veritable writer's block and I picked up the book, read a chapter on prayer, and returned to the writing races, blueberry brain and all! What good news.

Then I thought of my youngest daughter because words make a difference, sacred speech travels the good news. After a washed out, terrible, horrible, no good, very bad Sunday, to paraphrase Judith Viorst in *Alexander and the Terrible, Horrible, No Good, Very Bad Day*, I slipped in the car and the sweet saint of a child reached over and touched my hand and spoke, "I just love it when you tell stories." What good news to hear on a bad news Sunday! Those kind words sent me flying through the roof with happiness and joy. Kindness, what good news! Sacred speech overflows with kindness, kind words, and kind thoughts. Be kind. It is a sacred act.

Oh, you want me to give you my three daughter's names? I cannot reveal their names, but I will tell you that all three went to Baylor University in Waco, Texas and all three are married. I will not reveal their names, but I will pray in sacred speech that God reveals His Name to you: *Thou art the Christ, the Son of the Living God; Healer of the Broken; Wonderful. Counselor, Mighty God, Everlasting Father, Prince of Peace.*

Sacred speech *overflows* **with kindness, kind words, and kind thoughts. Be kind. It is a** *sacred* **act.**

Well, midnight has arrived. The rain stopped. Pinkish, purplish clouds appeared. Night drifted and darkness settled in. Crickets chirp outside. A fluttering moth keeps banging into the screen over the window behind me trying to reach the light. Rain drips off the roof and I imagine for a moment that I am on that green swing and the North Carolina porch angling toward sacred space while the rain drips off the roof and a bird nests in the bushes near the porch.

Can you feel the cool mountain air on your face? Do you hear the birds singing hymns? Do you see the lightning bugs blinking? What about the cicadas dancing and singing in unison a chorus of worship? And all is well. Yes, all is well. Goodnight. Get some rest. I pray all is well with you, that the chaos has surrendered to Peace. Tomorrow, we journey into the art of the sacred ear.

The Sacred Ear
FROM FOLLY TO WISDOM

"We are all in the same boat. We must pin our hopes on the mercy of God and the work of Christ, not our own goodness."

~C. S. Lewis, *Reflections on the Psalms*[44]~

---

44   C. S. Lewis, *Reflections on the Psalms* (London: Harcourt Brace & Company, 1958), 13.

"Do you know how to use these?" The pharmacist asked me if I knew how to put drops in my ear when I picked up my prescription.

"Well, yes ma'am, I guess," I replied thinking what a strange thing to ask a grown man.

"Be careful," she said as she reiterated, "Place the drops carefully in your ear and be sure to follow the directions. Put the drops in your ear three times a day. Have a good day."

She smiled. She had a pretty smile and seemed to enjoy her job. Enjoyment of a job does not register in many places I go. And, besides, what man does not follow directions, ask for directions, and seek directions in taking medicine, traveling, and working a job?

I totally forgot about the pharmacist until a few days later. Early one morning I finished my shower, dressed, combed my hair, brushed my teeth, forgot to put drops in my ear, and, just as I was about to race out the door, decided to put some moistening drops in my eyes because they felt dry. I wear contacts and moistening the eyes is not an unusual thing. *Be careful. Follow directions.*

I grabbed the drops in a rush, opened my right eye, dropped the teardrops gently in my eye, and felt an unfamiliar sensation. I looked at the small white bottle as my eye burned. I had picked up the wrong bottle. I dropped ear drops in my right eye. My foolish act led to an immediate scramble. I turned on the water faucet over the sink, cupped my hands under the water, splashed water in my right eye, blinked about a hundred times, and waited to go blind.

The burning sensation subsided. I gained my composure, read the eye drop bottle in small letters with big, hard to grasp words that seemed to all end in *"ate"* like sulfate and *"ine"* like anti-pyrine.

I caution you here against two things: One, I caution you against Googling the dangers and side effects of the ear drops that numb pain in the middle ear. The danger read with clarity: *Do not place in mouth or eyes.* The side effects read with equal clarity: burning sensation, redness, new pain in and around the ear, and possible, though not likely, dizziness. Do not, I say, Google something like this because sometimes in life it is best not to know. The mind does funny things to the brain.

Second, do not learn the ancient Greek. *Anti* means "against" and *pyrine* struck a chord in my brain indicating our English word pyre. The word *pyre* in Greek refers to *pura* which means a pile of burning material such as wood. If you pick up a copy of the Greek historian Herodotus (Fourth century B.C.) you will find the he uses the word *pura* as a pyre upon which King Cyrus of Persia had built so that he could inflame and burn his enemy Croesus.[45]

A pyre indicates a fire. Now you know why I thought I would go blind when I did that foolish act of dripping "anti-fire" ear drops in my right eye that caused a burning fire in my eye. If I was not Croesus on the pyre would I not at least be Samson whose blinded eyes prevented him from seeing the destruction soon to come when he pulled down the pillars in the Dagon temple? Do not, I repeat, learn ancient Greek. It too can cause the brain to twist normal words and confuse the brain. A confused mind increases the potential for foolishness.

If all this seems dramatic, it was. The fire in my eye dissipated as the cool water washed my right eye clean, fresh so that I could see again and hear again.

"Hear again," you ask?

---

45 Herodotus, *The Persian Wars* I.86.

I wear contacts and occasionally I say or hear someone say, "I need to put my glasses on so I can hear."

Hearing is seeing. And seeing helps hearing, so to speak, certainly if you look into the scriptures. What you find is that hearing and seeing fit closely together like pieces of a puzzle or like stiches in a patchwork quilt.

Consider Job's (13:1) lament, "My eyes have seen all this, my ears have seen and heard it." Or the psalmist's wailing cry, "Lord, you have seen all this! Do not be silent!" (Psalm 35:22). The writer of proverbs spins wisdom in hearing and seeing, "My son, if you accept my words and store up my commands within you, turning your ear to wisdom and applying your heart to understanding, and if you call out for insight and cry aloud for understanding, and if you look for it as for silver and search for it as for hidden treasure, then you will understand the fear of the Lord and find the knowledge of God. For

> **Hearing is seeing. And seeing helps hearing, so to speak...**

the Lord gives wisdom, and from his mouth come knowledge and understanding" (Proverbs 2:1-6).

The prophet Isaiah thundered that a day would come when people would hear and not understand, see yet never perceive, a time when calloused hearts would refuse to hear and close their eyes (Isaiah 6:10). Healing comes through seeing, hearing, and attaching it to God's wisdom in the echo of His whispers, His still small voice.

Time calls for sacred space in the aftermath of sacred silence and sacred speech which then spawns the art of the sacred ear, "...otherwise they might see with their eyes, hear with their ears, understand with their hearts, and turn and be healed" (Isaiah 6:10).

Even John exiled on the isle of Patmos repeats in his vision, "He who has an ear, let him hear." He then hears "a loud voice in heaven," describes what he sees (a dragon!), gives insight into a spiritual battle (this calls for patient endurance and faithfulness on the part of the saints), and exclaims again, "He who has an ear, let him hear," while adding in the aftermath of his exclamation, "This calls for wisdom" (Revelation 13:9, 18).

Hearing God's voice, seeing God's vision for your own life, and finding wisdom in a world of folly requires the ultimate sacred space, the art of using your ears and eyes to impact the heart on the path to wisdom.

When Henry David Thoreau wrote his famous book *Walden*, or *Life in the Woods*, subtitled *On the Duty of Civil Disobedience* in August of 1854, he penned a chapter on the bean-field. Early in his book he spoke of time, its haste, fury, and ceaseless ticking to pressure mankind and said of mankind, "He [she] has no time to be anything but a machine."[46] Writing of the bean field Thoreau warns, "Ancient poetry and mythology suggest, at least, that husbandry [farming] was once a sacred art; but it is pursued with irreverent haste and heedlessness by us, our object being to have large farms and large crops merely."[47] Thoreau continues by saying, "The true husbandman [farmer] will cease from anxiety..."[48]

If farming is a sacred art when set in time and enjoyed in the simplicity of its task rather than a race against time in the throes of anxiety, selfishness, greed, and a quest for the largest and

---

46 Henry David Thoreau, *Walden, and On the Duty of Civil Disobedience* (New York: Franklin Watts, 1854), 5.

47 Thoreau, *Walden*, 95.

48 Thoreau, *Walden*, 96.

best crop ever, the sacredness of the art of farming becomes a feast of joy. In similar fashion, if the art of the sacred ear becomes a sacred art set in time and enjoyed in the simplicity of its practice rather than a race against time in the throes of anxiety, selfishness, greed, and a quest for conquering the idea of God, life, and sacred space, the sacredness of the art of the sacred ear becomes a feast of joy thrusting you into life with God's peace.

In other words, slow down, *create* **sacred space, rehearse sacred silence,** *flex the soul* **in the exercise of two-fold sacred speech, and** *practice* **the sacred art of the listening ear.**

In other words, slow down, create sacred space, rehearse sacred silence, flex the soul in the exercise of two-fold sacred speech, and practice the sacred art of the listening ear. Frank W. Moyle in *The Book of Uncommon Prayer* names this as a vital aspect of the interior life: "reflection."[49] Often life is like a rough sea, to paraphrase Moyle, and a person can never find time to be still to reflect on anything.

---

49   Moyle, *Book of Uncommon Prayer*, 30.

Moyle emphasizes reflection by noting, "Now reflection is a very different function from thinking. Thinking is an activity of the mind; reflection is its passivity."[50] Moyle continues, "Modern man [woman] is inclined to regard this as a waste of time, and so he carries his everlasting hustle and business into his interior life until there is such a conflict there that he cannot—and sometimes complains because he cannot—call his soul his own."[51]

In the throes of ministry and career, three times I moved to the edge of overload near collapse, and taxed emotionally in the hyper-connected world of ministry. The first two times planned sabbaticals arrived just in time to save the day so that I could recharge my batteries and allow my body, soul, and mind to reunite. Do not overanalyze the last statement. The bottom line is that my exhausted body needed rest, my weary soul needed sacred space, and my mind needed time for new reflection, a fresh vision from God so that I could effectively serve God in the future.

On the third experience at the edge of overload, and my most recent, I felt something in

---

50   Moyle, *Book of Uncommon Prayer*, 30.

51   Moyle, *Book of Uncommon Prayer*, 30.

the interior life I had never felt before. I sensed an overarching sense, to use Moyle's words, that my soul was not my own.

I remembered a seminary professor once saying over thirty years ago, "Be careful in ministry not to become a slave to ministry but rather a servant in the ministry." I did not feel a sense of freedom to do what God had called me to do, to be myself in service to Christ, and to serve people as Christ called me in humility, grace, and with Christ's peace. My interior life had transposed a false spirit of joy, when, in fact, I felt miserable on the inside. My soul's interior had arrived as a ship sailing on a journey of rough sea, my sails being ripped by the folly around me, my ship being tossed and thrashed like a bottle violently tossed and churned in the tumultuous, white capped waters of a storm.

Moyle advised me to stop for reflection, to turn my imagination toward Christ ("the focusing of the imagination on Christ"), to repent (*metavoia* in Greek, "change your thinking"), and to embrace "a new mentality."[52] Moyle's wisdom provided a warning signal for me. He talked of the Pharisee that Jesus boasted he was not like other men and

---

52 Moyle, *Book of Uncommon Prayer*, 36.

"prayed thus with himself" (Luke 18:11, NKJV). Moyle warned, "That is why there is so much selfishness abroad in the world: there are too many people using their imagination wrongly, praying with themselves instead of with God or turning the mirror inward to reflect upon themselves instead of outward to reflect His image."[53] How had I missed this all these years?

Often in the folly of our selfish praying and attempts at listening to God we focus on ourselves, turning our inward mirror on ourselves, and feel an overwhelming sense of self-pity, exhaustion, weariness, and, in the process, become a slave of time, a slave to what we do, and chained to life rather than free to live the life Christ intended. We focus the mirror of *our image* like a Pharisee praying to himself, boastful, prideful, and restless rather than reflecting *His image* of humility, grace, and peace.

The art of the sacred ear requires turning our imagination toward Christ, reflecting on Him, and listening with our ears and heart for what God has for us in that moment or in future days. I will refer to this as spiritual *acoustics*.

---

53 Moyle, *Book of Uncommon Prayer*, 32.

Two words speak of the listening ear in the Bible. One word is "to hear," *akouo* in Greek, which means to hear like hearing the rustling of leaves from the wind, or a sound that goes bump in the night and arrests your senses, or a voice that speaks, cries, moans, or whines. Think of acoustics as the sound in a room that enters your ear.

The art of the sacred ear demands that you listen to God, hear His voice through His Word, and welcome His voice into the soul, into the interior life to claim it as your own. On the one hand, "faith comes by hearing and hearing by the Word of God" (Romans 10:17). On the other hand, Jesus instructed his hearers in the parable of the seed and the soils (of the heart), "He who has ears to hear, let him hear" (*akouo*, Mark 4:9).

If we return to Thoreau's comment of husbandry or farming as a sacred art, the art of the listening ear like farming requires plowing, sowing seeds, watering, sunning, waiting, and reaping of the harvest. Simply put, farming cannot be rushed, hastened, fast-forwarded, but has to take place in its time, according to the seasons, and according to the patience necessary for the soil, sun, rain, and crop to ripen to fruition. Simply put, the art of the listening ear ceases from anxiety, refrains from haste, repents, reflects, and ripens to a fresh vision of Christ in the interior life. The fresh vision supplies spiritual refreshment that supplants a lack of spiritual vitality and provides new spiritual energy.

The second word used in the Bible that speaks of the listening ear is the word *upak-ouo*, "to hear under," or what is commonly referred to in Scripture as obedience. "What manner of man is this! The winds and the sea obey (*upakouo*) Him!" the disciples exclaimed of Jesus (Luke 8:25).

A follower of Christ who possesses *knowledge* **of God obeys God, hears and** *responds* **to what God desires.**

Christ learned obedience even by the things he suffered (Hebrews 5:8). Every thought of ours is to be taken captive to the obedience of Christ (2 Corinthians 10:5). A follower of Christ who possesses knowledge of God obeys God, hears and responds to what God desires (2 Thessalonians 1:8; 3:14). The art of the sacred ear involves a reflection that hears God and responds in obedience to God's desires. If *akouo* means "to hear the knock on the door," and it does, then *upakouo* means "to answer the door." The art of the sacred ear hears Christ knock on the door and answers the door to hear what God will say.

No wonder John's vision on the isle of Patmos included a clear message from Jesus, "Here I am! I stand at the door and knock. If anyone hears (*akouo*) my voice and opens the door, I will come in and eat with him, and he with me" (Revelation 3:20). The art of the sacred ear results in fresh fellowship with Jesus likened unto a banquet meal, a feast of fellowship and delight.

In *Symposium*, Plato writes of a banquet, a festive meal where friends gathered and shared wisdom among hearty dialogue and scholarly philosophical discussion.[54] Jesus, Paul, and John in Revelation each spoke of a meal where disciples and friends share fellowship among words of wisdom. Of Jesus, He invited the disciples to a banqueting meal of bread and wine in the shadow and wisdom of the cross (Luke 22:20). Of the apostle Paul he challenged each member of the church to participate in the seriousness of examining him or herself in the wisdom of the Lord's Supper, a thanksgiving meal (I Corinthians 11:25). Of John

---

54 Plato, *Symposium* 174a.

exiled on Patmos, he proposed the invitation of wisdom where Christ would join the saints in a banquet of joy, peace, and glory where Christ as Wisdom would be the honored guest as well as the ultimate servant (Revelation 3:20). The art of the sacred ear gives pause to look into Christ's eyes, propose a toast to his glory, and wait with ears ready to devour and digest the wisdom of His every word.

One key to devouring and digesting the wisdom of Christ encompasses waiting before the Lord in His presence, waiting before listening to Christ. Jeremiah's poetic lament provides wisdom for us here: "I say to myself, 'The Lord is my portion; therefore I will wait for him.' The Lord is good to those whose hope is in him, to the one who seeks him; it is good to wait quietly for the salvation of the Lord" (Lamentations 3:24-26).

Waiting may yet prove the hardest chore. The mind wanders, drifts, solves puzzles totally unsolvable, debates itself, and congratulates itself while forgetting what it sought in the first place. A wandering mind must be trained to angle toward sacred space and the sacred ear like a fisherman dropping the wormed bait on a hook and lowering the hook and line into the water to wait with expectation for the tug at the line and red and white cork to bob and go under. The fisherman waits, enjoys the scenery while looking around, and anticipates catching fish with the excitement of fireworks on July 4th. A good fisherman knows how to wait with patience, anticipation, and hope.

> **A good fisherman** *knows* **how to wait with patience,** *anticipation,* **and hope.**

God's wisdom flows as the wisdom upon which you wait, wonder, and worship. His wisdom instills humility. His wisdom captures wonder, bottles it in your soul, and releases it like endorphins in the brain after a hard physical work or exercise. His wisdom influences daily decision-making, choices and paths you choose to travel. His wisdom forgives sin and causes you to learn from past sins so as not to repeat them, and to grow from mistakes so to flower with a fresh scent.

His wisdom anticipates life. Jesus said, "I have come that you might have life and have it more abundantly" or "to the full" (John 10:10). Wisdom acknowledges life in its ups and downs, unexpected twists and turns like a winding river, and in its rises and falls. Wisdom accepts the fact that you cannot know everything, nor should you try or even act like you know everything.

Henry David Thoreau describes the beauty, hues, distinct features, and undulating cascades of the water's ripple at Walden Pond. Over the course of the four seasons the rain, snow, ice, and greenish-blue tint of the pond's water he explains the shoreline and the rise and fall of the of the pond. Thoreau said, "The pond rises and falls, but whether regularly or not, and within what period, nobody knows, though, as usual, many pretend to know."[55]

Life comes at you daily and yearly in a series of rises and falls and some will be known and understood, while others will arrive at your doorstep and you will not have the faintest clue as to the rise or fall. *You* or *many* may act like you know or pretend to know and attempt to explain the rise and fall, but sometimes it simply pays, if you will, to go with the flow, focus, not on the rise and fall, but on the Christ's Living water, His sustaining strength, and His sacred provision.

The sacred ear guides you to listen to God's wisdom for help in the falls. God's wisdom

55 Thoreau, *Walden*, 104.

humbles you to appreciation in the rises. The sacred ear helps you stay balanced. Mostly, you learn at God's feet in the wait and in His wisdom that worry accomplishes almost nothing and that worship magnifies His goodness and that life cannot always be figured out. Life, for all its worth, means that you live and you cannot control the fall and rise of life's pond or stop the sun or rain any more than you can put a leaf back on a tree after it falls. After all, the old Presbyterian preacher George A. Buttrick once allayed, "Life is a series of events to be lived through rather than an intellectual riddle to be played with and solved."[56] This is wisdom.

Paul's doxology in a Roman world of tragedy, complexity, and folly addresses wisdom through poetry: "Oh, the depth of the riches and wisdom and knowledge of God! How unsearchable his judgments, and his paths beyond tracing out! Who has known the mind of the Lord? Or who has been his counselor? Who has ever given to God, that God should repay him? For of him and through and to him are all things. To Him be glory forever and ever! Amen!" (Romans 11:33-36, *NIV*). Paul sums it up. God gives wisdom, but some

---

56   As quoted by Paul Powell in *Gospel for the Graveside* (Tyler: Texas: Paul Powell, Inc., 1981), 46.

days you can no more fathom God or trace out His paths any more than you could find a penny dropped to the bottom of Walden Pond. But you can admire His beauty, hues, distinct features, and undulating cascades of Living Water and rest in Him.

"Come to me, all you who are weary and burdened, and I will give you rest. Take my yoke upon you and learn from me, for I am gentle and humble in heart, and you will find rest for your souls" (Matthew 11:28-29). "Rest" indicates repose, an intermission, or refreshment much like a vacation at the beach. God's wisdom compels us to turn to Jesus to find rest and lessen the noise, chaos, and folly of life.

Can noise, however soft or loud, ever be totally shut out? Can the tide of chaos be fully stemmed or stopped? Can folly, in its insidious foolishness and boastful pride, though, be completely avoided?

Even as I write the world spins in apparent noise, chaos, and folly. The world whirls, almost out of control. War escalates in the Middle East between Israel and Hamas, Jerusalem and Gaza, missiles flying overhead while children attend school and people eat lunch at restaurants. In the

Ukraine a rocket launcher blasts a passenger airplane and it falls out of the sky into a war zone
making it difficult for rescue workers and hu-
manitarian aid workers. Soldiers in Afghanistan
and Iraq avoid daily improvised explosive devices
(IED) buried in the ground undetected and clandestine beneath the sand. Soldiers, both men and
women, die in combat, many survive with wounds
and scars not to be forgotten. The art of the sacred
ear leans in and moves us toward God to make
sense of the insensible and to understand the mis-
understood and to anchor life in the world storms
and the rises and falls which appear unavoidable
and often cloaked in folly.

As I write I think of the church, maybe your
church and my church, and maybe not your church
or mine, but the church enmeshed in so much folly
and trying to escape it with the hilarity of a circus
clown, or the frustration of a woman who walked
into a spider web and trying to remove the spider
web from her face while simultaneously scream-
ing for fear of the black widow spider. The church
of the 21st century, which resembles a board of
directors rather than the body of Christ, seems
more concerned for bottom line business than the
mind of Christ, angles toward building structure

than building the people of God, and applauds gimmicks and proud displays rather than prayer, spiritual disciplines, and dependence on God for its sustenance, strength, and ministry.

I wonder if maybe a game of competition ensues today inside churches and between churches, and strenuous efforts and untold energy is given to domination rather than service. Jealousy, pettiness, Pharisaism, competition, anger, and other such impediments, which I call the church game, have caused us to miss the fundamental call and cause of Christ for the world, the church, and for hurting people. The art of the sacred ear invites us back to Christ, Christian basics, and spiritual disciplines that sprinkle the rain of God's wisdom into our hearts.

> **I wonder if maybe a game of** *competition* **ensues today inside churches and between churches, and** *strenuous* **efforts and untold energy is given to** *domination* **rather than service.**

I served as a pastor for over 30 years and serve as an interim pastor today. One day in frustration I said to my mother, "Mom, what I entered the ministry to do, serve Christ, has turned into nothing more than meetings, keeping the church board happy, managing the church staff of which many seemed unhappy, and maintaining church life in its hectic pace rather than ministry, reaching people for Christ, and proclaiming the good news of the gospel of Christ in his great wisdom for life itself."

Remember that deacon who told me once, "I need you to start acting like a CEO and less like a pastor!" Oh what folly the church often embraces, encounters, and enchants as if the answer to church growth and life finds resolve in man's schemes. I fear we rely more on man's plans than God's. Worse yet, I fear I rely on my own ingenuity rather than God's genius and His sovereignty. The art of the sacred ear allows me to weed out the garden, to separate the wheat from the chaff, to focus on the true seed of the Gospel, and to bear fruit for God's glory for the church and for my own life.

I love the church, churches, and every church I have pastored and almost felt like not saying anything critical of the church. I mean, sacred space should reduce a critical spirit within you and plant flowering seeds of the fruit of the spirit: love, joy, peace, patience, kindness, goodness, faithfulness, gentleness, and self-control (Galatians 5:22-23).

However, only when the church, its leaders and people humbly bow before Christ and return to His sacredness will the church flourish in the eyes of God. Our success models for building churches has diminished the sacred hour of worship, the sacred heart, and the sacred thrust of quietness, peace, and wisdom in Christ. The art of listening to the still small voice of God will instill in Christians, Christian leaders, and servants of Christ a desire to please God, to eradicate folly, and seek God's wisdom in building a church to His glory and honor.

On a personal level, so much noise, chaos, and folly happen. Research reveals that a world of technology, sensors, and electronics will change the way we see, hear, think, feel, and live. Already this is happening as cell phones, computers, and sensory capacitors like cameras can transmit you in real time from your home to places like England when you travel, to Afghanistan where soldiers fight, or to your daughter's living room in Houston, Texas.

The implications for sensory overload, connectivity in extremis, the invasion of privacy, and restlessness in a sensor-driven world appear real, stressful, and an unintended consequence of less down time and more pressure for the average human being. According to Gershom Dublon and Joseph Paradiso in *The Scientific American*, "For many people, ourselves included, the world we just described has the potential to be frightening." They ask, "Is this a dream or a nightmare?"[57] Add to this the routine, unexpected, shocking, and sometimes stultifying horrors of life and the potential fright arrives like a ghost in the night.

In more recent days, these events took place: of the routine...going to the grocery store or dropping the kids off at soccer or even trying to have a meeting at work proved a challenge because of cell phone calls, ear buds, and texting; of the unexpected...a Wichita Falls, Texas man, a street worker for the city works in a culvert only to feel the sting of over a thousand bee stings in an ambush of bees, rats show up at the museum the *Louvre* in Paris, a bat shows up in my attic at my house, and mice leave their dropping as invaders

---

57 Gershom Dublon and Joseph A. Paradiso, "Extra Sensory Perception," *ScientificAmerican.com* (July 2014): 41.

in my father's house in the North Carolina mountains; of the shocking...a retired pastor drives into a mall parking lot and sets himself on fire because he feels he has not done enough for God or humanity, or an errant missile hits the wrong target in Gaza and children die innocently; and of the stultifying horrors...four plane crashes in seven days, tornadoes, hurricanes, minor tremors and earthquakes, and the proverbial clean up from car crashes, school shootings, and tsunamis. Imagine, and this is just the evening news.

What time, what person, what Christian cannot see the need for creating sacred space and sacred silence to move from noise to quiet, from chaos to peace, from folly to wisdom, to at least gain some balance for your life? To at least find coping for the present routines, unexpected events, shocking things, and stultifying horrors that affect each of us daily? To at least approach the future with hope and not despair? To at least find solace in the soul in solitude at the security of Christ? To at least find refuge in God in the raging war within or on the outside? To at least sensitize the soul for God's good things in a world where so many hyper-sensory messages bombard and so many bad things overpower the emotions?

Jesus said, "Peace I leave with you; my peace I give to you. I do not give as the world gives. Do not let your hearts be troubled and do not be afraid" (John 14:27, *NIV*). Jesus encouraged saints with hope in the woeful shadows of a troubled world, "I have told you these things so that in me you may have peace. In this world you will have trouble. But take heart! I have overcome the world" (John 16:33, *NIV*). For greater is He that is in you than he who is in the world! (I John 4:4). Sacred space and the sacred ear push aside the shadows of despair, hopelessness, and trouble and awaken you to the light of God's comfort, peace, strength, power, and wisdom for the daily grind.

The art of the sacred ear provides wisdom, but also produces within you refreshment with soul cleansing. In the art of the sacred ear you listen for the still small voice of God. To listen you sit on the porch, wait quietly in a chair in a room, shut off the stereo in the car, and/or take a technology break by shutting out all computers, phones, and other means of technology that might keep you from reflecting on Christ for the moment.

Around you, if I paraphrase the prophet Elijah when the Lord passed by, you will hear a multitude of sounds: you might hear the whipping, whistling winds, the shattering of rocks, the rattling of windows as the ground splits beneath you in an earthquake, the crackling and raging of a fire, or a million other noises in the swirling chaos and surrounding folly (I Kings 19:11-12). Reflect and tune the listening ear to the voice of God, His still small voice, His gentle whisper. Stop; mark that moment as sacred because God speaks as we listen in the freedom of sacred space.

What will God say? He loves you. He speaks righteousness, grace, and peace. He speaks forgiveness, both His and the necessary practice of forgiveness for you in relations and for personal healing. He unfolds the joy of the fruit of His Spirit. He reveals His plans for His servants. His small voice, whispers, seldom shouts, and His gentleness broods over you like the coolness of a fog over a pond on a cool morning while you stand on the shore barefoot in the dew as the sun rises. A cool breeze, a freshness, almost a cleanliness or cleansing effect washes over you. Sacred space in the power of the sacred ear cleanses you and prepares you for new vision, new vistas, and new action for service in glory to God. It equips you to act and live by God's wisdom in the right heart, speech, and service.

On the morning of May 18, 1980, Mount St. Helen's, a volcano in Washington State, erupted. The massive spurts of fire, lava, and ashes spewed towering plumes of smoke and toxic fumes into the morning sky. Fifty-seven people died and more than 200 square miles of land and forests were ambushed. Imagine a fire of devastation demolishing homes, trees, wildlife, and stripping a mountain of trees and foliage, barren, black, beaten down by the fire's dragon-like blow torch. The explosive

Sacred space in the *power* **of the sacred ear cleanses you and** *prepares* **you for new vision, new vistas, and new action for service in** *glory to God.*

ferocity of force left the land like a petrified forest and a nearby lake devoid of much activity, ghost-like, alone in its eeriness. According to McKenzie Funk in *National Geographic Magazine,* a rebirth occurred after the volcano largely due to "biological legacies"–fallen trees, buried roots, seeds, gophers, amphibians–that survived the blast thanks to the snow, topography, or luck."[58]

Thirty years later the region flourishes more vibrant than ever: flowers abloom, trees bearing green leaves, animals racing fleet of foot, even trout, longer than ever, swimming in the nearby lake. Foliage spread, brilliant and vibrant colors dotted the landscape as if a painter splattered the canvas, and life brimmed afresh where once steamy black ash smoldered the dew of death. One man described one piece of the land after the volcano 30 years later, as "a runaway horse," vibrant, alive, free, fresh, and breathing in the freshness of each new day while traversing the plains.[59] One theory, it seems, is that the fire, ashes, and death that the volcano delivered in its explosion, in the end added nutrients to the land and bust evolved to burst into a panoramic, miraculous, colorful rebirth.

The phenomenon of Mount St. Helen's reminded me of an escape to find sacred space at my

---

58 McKenzie Funk, "Mountain Transformed: Thirty Years after the Blast, Mount St. Helen's is Reborn Again," *National Geographic Magazine* (May 2010): 38-52.

59 McKenzie Funk, "Mountain Transformed: Thirty Years after the Blast, Mount St. Helen's is Reborn Again," *National Geographic Magazine* (May 2010): 49.

friend's ranch overlooking the Brazos River near my home in Texas. The frantic pace and pressure of ministry needed time for sacred space, silence, speech, and the listening ear. As I drove onto the ranch property I noticed a fire in the field on that spring morning.

Rather than drive straight to the cabin along the dirt road, I drove to the ranch house and found my friend, the ranch manager.

"Hey," I said with the frantic voice of a man in panic in search of a fire truck to put out a fire, "you have a fire near the front gate! You better call the fire department. Orange flames are shooting upward."

He laughed and said, "Calm down. It's okay, it's a controlled fire. It's agricultural burning. We burn off the coastal, the riff-raff. We burn the land to prepare it for planting season."

"Oh," I replied as I stored that thought for pondering and reflecting upon at a later date. Like Mount St. Helen's, my friend's ranch land experienced a cleansing as if by fire and a soil prepared for future foliage, fruit, and a flowering vibrancy.

Think of the art of the sacred ear as the transformation after the volcanic blast, the rebirth after the ashes, the greening of the heart and soul after the fire, and the renewal of the spirit to prepare it for future service for Christ and to people. Think of the art of the sacred ear as the sounds, "acoustics" or *akouo*, "to hear," that lead to reflection on Christ and prepare you to serve Christ in a fresh, new way daily and forever. The art of the sacred ear surrenders *akouo* (hear) to *upakouo* ("to hear under," or "obey") so that you seek to please Christ in action and speech. Remember, Christ knocks on the door (*akouo*) and you have to open it (*upakouo*), that is, obey Him through service.

The sacred ear thrusts us toward Christ in reflection and moves us to honor and please God by work in His service. Paul prays for the Colossian Christians with these words: "...that you may live a life worthy of the Lord and please Him in every way, bearing fruit in every good work (*ergon*), according to the knowledge [wisdom and understanding] of God..." (Colossians 1:10, *NIV*).

The word "work" (*ergon* in Greek) defines a function or action, according to the physician of the Roman court and emperor (A.D. 129-199) who wrote *Methods of Medicine*.[60] For example, an eye functions for seeing; a brain functions for thinking; a vein for transporting blood, and an ear

---

60 Galen, *On the Natural Faculties* I.2.6.

for hearing. Each natural faculty in the body has a function producing action. Similarly, the spiritual faculties, namely the heart, mind, and soul function to produce Christian action. The art of the sacred ear, hearing God's call, voice, and understanding His heart lead to right and proper Christian action. Christian reflection produces Christlike action.

Do you see how important the art of the sacred ear can be for your personal life? The 16th century's St. John of the Cross said, "All the soul ever longed for is intimacy with God."[61] The sacred ear reflects in such a way that the soul develops intimacy with God that leads to acts of compassion and ministry toward

> **A desire to** *please* **God and practice His presence in the real world** *precedes* **action.**

others. After all, as the 17th century Carmelite friar known as Brother Lawrence once remarked in a letter, "One does not become holy all at once."[62]

---

61 St. John of the Cross, *Dark Night of the Soul* (transl. by Mirabi Starr; London: Riverhead Books, 2002), 179.

62 Nicholas Herman, *The Practice of the Presence of God: Conversations and Letters of Brother Lawrence* (Oxford: Oneworld, 1692; reprint, 2000), 87.

He calls prayer and action the practice of the presence of God, having said, "That we should feed and nourish our souls with high notions of God, which would yield us great joy in being devoted to Him."[63]

The writer Flannery O'Connor in *A Prayer Journal* shapes one final thought in the art of the sacred ear that listens in the shadows to the still small voice of God. Reflection leads to action, that is, reflection focuses on Christ and all that He is and wishes to be in you. A desire to please God and practice His presence in the real world precedes action (*ergon*). O'Connor's journal describes this best when she carved these words in ink, quite possibly also in her heart, "I do not know you God because I am in the way. Please help me to push myself aside. Dear God send me your grace."[64] Reflection in the art of the sacred ear pushes the self aside, making way for the refreshing rain of God's grace that supplies you with wisdom, power, and grace to serve others in actions of good work (*ergon*, Colossians 1:10).

---

63   Herman, *The Practice of the Presence of God*, 9.

64   Flannery O'Connor, *A Prayer Journal* (New York: Farrar, Straus, and Giroux, 2013), 3, 28.

Author's Note to the Reader

Dear reader, as I arrived at the end of writing this chapter I must share two items with you. First, I felt sadness. The kind of sadness you feel when the blahs and blues hover over your heart like winter depression. Ernest Hemingway once quipped in a letter, "The terrible mood of depression of whether it is any good or not is what is known as the Artist's Reward."[65]

I wondered if you felt the sadness toward the end or maybe heaviness in the chapter as I talked about the importance of reflection versus the challenge of it while discussing along the way the folly in the world, in the church, and in the self against the wonders of God's wisdom? The art of the sacred ear, in its result, like Thoreau's bean-field should yield a crop of joy, a release from the slavery of depression, and restore hope in God, humanity, and even the world.

I must a second item share with you. This chapter, should I say this, proved gut-wrenching, perplexing, an amalgamation of hard-scrabble words that seemed, at times, difficult to pen and find the right words. It was a chapter of rough

---

65 Phillips, ed., *Ernest Hemingway on Writing*, 52.

seas and one sleepless night while writing. One moment I wrestled with God like Jacob at the Ford of the Jabbok River. I limped along trying to find the right word at each given moment on the blank page.

On another occasion I tangled with the sea itself, like Hemingway's *Old Man and The Sea*, the old man fighting the foaming sea and trying to deliver the big, angry fish to the boat in a conquest of human will and ingenuity. In writing this chapter, I felt a sense of urgency as if I were rushed and running for my life like people in the running of the bulls in the San Fermin Festival in Pamplona, Spain.

The rushed urgency, as you well know, was the opposite of what I describe in *Sacred Space*, albeit this chapter on the art of the sacred ear. Need I say it again? Sacred space and the art of the sacred ear present a plea for a simplified approach to life at times and for a slower pace at which to enjoy life and appreciate the blessings of life. It generates time for reflection, which as I described and we observed, is not thinking but reflection, a turning of the imagination, heart, soul, and mind toward Christ who calms the rough seas of a troubled heart.

Oh, I should also tell you about the weather. Dear reader, it is still July in Texas as I write. This chapter has taken the better part of a month. Hemingway wrote *The Torrents of Spring* in ten days, mind you. Fiction writer Stephen King says you should be able to write a good book in three months, thinking of course, of seasons as writing seasons for another project.

Henry David Thoreau lived at Walden Pond, the serene, placid, tranquil lake in Concord, Massachusetts, for two years, two months, and two days. Apparently, he wrote, drafted, rewrote, and perfected his book Walden from 1847 until 1854 when it was finally published–seven trying, taxing years.

From all I can tell, since I am not an expert on Thoreau or Walden, writing the book, his travels, and his health issues (he died of tuberculosis in 1862) apparently slowed and dried his writing and his production as a writer dwindled in his later years. I wonder if the realization of nature's voice, his brief stint in jail in those years, and his encounters with nature, life, and mankind diminished his desire to write?

Trust me, I have not forgotten. I am telling you about the weather when I was writing this chapter. The hour right now is 12:18 a.m. The night radiates with stars twinkling and sparkling in against a dark sky like fireflies buzzing and blinking. Earlier this evening a beautiful sunset in an act of pure laziness drifted in a fire-flame of orange below the horizon as it shot hues of magenta, pink, and orange into the darkening sky. I watched it all from the white, wooden rocking chair on the back porch while tree leaves wisped in the wind and whispered amid a gentle breeze.

However, earlier this morning, it rained. I mean, here it is July and the last two days the temperature rose to over 100 degrees, so hot you could fry eggs, or poach them if you please, on my driveway. But right before noon, the sun faded and the sky softened from blue to gray, and the heavens opened their buckets, and rain poured on my house, yard, and the streets and cars in the distance. The rain splashed the roof, rushed through the gutters like a river tumbling the waters, and sprinkled the earth with showers of blessing.

I sat in that white rocking chair and watched the theater of God's creation, to paraphrase Augustine; while the wind picked up, the leaves shook on the trees, birds darted for cover, and suddenly, surprisingly, seven deer and two light brown, white-speckled fawns leapt and raced through the field that used to be a ranch behind my house. The mist of rain refreshed my face as I observed the deer racing to who knows where as the force of the rain increased in speed and density, force and fury.

> **I listened and I think I** *heard* **the grass and trees clap their hands and** *shout,* **"Glory!"**

I listened, refreshed in the moment frozen in time, and witnessed creation's splendor exalting both earth and heaven. I listened as there is no sound as peaceful as the sound of rain. I listened and I think I heard the grass and trees clap their hands and shout, "Glory!" I listened and thanked God for a July rain, an unusual event in a Texas summer.

I observed nature: the clouds easing toward each other like friends; birds drinking in the rain, so to speak; the grapevine that twisted and ran along the barbed wire fence in my back yard, then vines up through limbs on my live oak tree, and vines dangling from the limbs, blowing and waving like floating scarves you would drape around your neck as you drove down the street with the car windows open. The stiff, humid air turned cooler as the weather cruised the skies.

I had a book in my lap while this Texas summer weather event surprised me with joy. I had just completed reading page 81 of Thoreau's Walden. The weather event, the moment isolated in my mind's eye, and the book converged in a surreal, sacred moment. Thoreau had asked, "What is the pill which will keep us well, serene, contented?"[66] His answer, so it seems to me, was... "undiluted morning air."[67] Thoreau then roared his prolific words like angels singing, "Morning air! If men will not drink of this at the fountainhead of the day, why, then, we must even bottle up some and sell it in the shops, for the benefit of those who have lost their subscription ticket to the morning time in this world."[68]

I suggest the morning air might be a good place and time to practice sacred space. And, alas, the rain subsided and the clouds gave way to a bright sun and the temperature rose from a cool 84 degrees Fahrenheit to a blistering 96 and all

---

66 Thoreau, *Walden*, 81.

67 Thoreau, *Walden*, 81.

68 Thoreau, *Walden*, 81.

was well. Yes, all was well. All is well. How about you? How is it with you? Is all well?

I talked about wisdom in this chapter, and worship, and not to worry, so to speak, but then I worried that you might think I was a weirdo or transcendentalist like Thoreau. A transcendentalist imagines ideals in the life that develop a philosophy that the transcendental and spiritual prove more important than the rational, material, and practical. The transcendentalist, although it is hard to pin this down in simple terms, generally believes in the human spirit as an independent source of wisdom and survival with instinctive, intuitive leanings, while preferring the distant God as opposed to the God close at hand. A transcendentalist I am not. Rather sacred space alerts the sacred ear that reflects on God in His wisdom in such a way that humility results, dependence on God follows, and a servant heart to encourage, assist, and join together with the body of Christ, people, and ministry to the needs of the world. The sacred ear equips you for service. Apart from the sacred ear there tends to be a missing of sacred moments and sacred opportunities for service.

Several years ago in Cambridge I walked through the stoned streets. I walked across a bridge as the sun rose high and the rays sparkled off the waters. The time was March 2003. A cool gentleness refreshed the morning air and happiness swirled around me. Flowers bloomed, danced, and dazzled in an array of colors much like I imagine at Walden Pond or in the garden at my father's house in the mountains of North Carolina or in your flower bed at home. A good mood swelled up in my heart and the people waltzing through the city center, the women riding their bikes, the tourists with maps and guides in hand, and professors and students off to the next tutoring session, all appeared well, at ease, at peace, in a kind of solemn, happy sacredness.

I turned right on Trinity Street and proceeded where it changed to King's Parade and eventually made my way through the crowd to a bookstore, *Waterstones*. As often I would do in Cambridge I glanced and perused bookshelves in search of wisdom, the attest earth-shattering book that would change my life, and fingered several while flipping through the pages.

On that day I selected an old book, a reprint of William Law's *A Serious Call to a Devout*

and Holy Life (1728). At the time I thought nothing of these book choices, but now I view this selection along with many others in Cambridge as sacred choices, sacred moments remembered, and later sacred treasure in their reading. I cannot remember much about Law's book except that I researched and discovered that he attended Emmanuel College in Cambridge, served as a priest, and challenged people of the day to practice the four steps of lectio divina, that is, divine or spiritual reading: read, meditate, rest in God's nearness, and live by the conduct in Christ based on the new understandings from ritual of the four steps. The sacred ear comes close to a combination of reflection, meditation, and resting in the nearness of Christ's heart and hand near the throne of grace.

William Law believed that every Christian ought to take seriously the Gospel of Christ and live a devout and holy life. He warned..."then how poorly must they perform their devotions, who are always in a hurry; who begin them in haste and hardly allow themselves to repeat their very form with any gravity or attention!"[69]

---

69 William Law, *A Serious Call to a Devout and Holy Life* (London: Vintage Books, 2002: reprint, England, 1728), 155.

Law referenced humility as one aim of our serious devotion in the call to a holy life. He named humility as "the dependent, helpless poverty of our state [mind]," anchored in the cross and humiliation of Christ, and as quality that helps us lest we "reason ourselves into all kinds of folly and misery..."[70]

Then Law signals a warning again, "Pride is only the disorder of the fallen world, it has no place amongst other beings; it can only subsist where ignorance and sensuality, lies and falsehood, lusts and impurity reign."[71]

The Oxford man who taught at Cambridge, C. S. Lewis, once followed Law's sentiment on pride calling it the opposite of humility and "the great sin."[72] Lewis said, "Pride leads to every other vice: it is the complete anti-God state of mind."[73] If pride is disorder and leads to every other vice then the art of the sacred ear embraces humility for the sake of killing pride one molecule at a time so that disorder is reordered under God's care and vice is forgiven by God's grace. Listening and

70 Law, *A Serious Call*, 189.

71 Law, *A Serious Call*, 191-92.

72 C. S. Lewis, *Mere Christianity* (New York: MacMillan Publishing, 1960: reprint edition 1943, 1945, 1952), 109.

73 Lewis, *Mere Christianity*, 109.

reflecting on Christ in the art of the sacred ear anchors us to the mind of Christ and prepares us for demonstrating God's care and showing His grace to others.

> **Listening and reflecting on *Christ* in the art of the sacred ear anchors us to the mind of Christ and *prepares* us for demonstrating God's care and showing His *grace* to others.**

I once knew a man who was proud of his pride. He boasted with a sly grin as an excuse for his awful behavior, "I have a problem with pride." What he really enjoyed was his pride, and I had not the guts to tell him, was his perceived power, his gamesmanship, his competitive spirit that congratulated him for his intelligence and superiority over others that allowed him to manipulate people and get his way by slight of hand and underground gossip.

"For, of course," C. S. Lewis said in discussing pride, "power is what Pride really enjoys: there is nothing that makes a man feel superior to others as being able to move them around like toy soldiers."[74] I am not sure why Lewis always capi-

---

74 Lewis, *Mere Christianity*, 110.

talized Pride in that section, except that maybe he recognized it as an important noun to name like naming an enemy or a disease that inflames the body. After all, Lewis again said, "For Pride is spiritual cancer: it eats up the very possibility of love, or contentment, or even common sense."[75]

If you think I was too harsh in describing the man's pride, let me tell you that the moment I heard him say that with his sinister smile, I knew myself capable of similar pride and, to paraphrase Jesus, I knew what was in man and woman and what was in me (John 2:25). Jesus often knew what was in the Pharisees with their plots, shyster schemes, gossipy talk, twists of his words, their lack of compassion for the masses, and their sinister pride. The sacred ear seeks to anchor your life to Christ, to destroy pride and Pharisaism, and to solidify love, contentment, common sense, and, more importantly, a sacred heart set on pleasing Christ. Beware, though, if you think you are not prideful or full of pride, it means you are very prideful indeed! The sacred ear moves you from the folly of pride to the faith, hope, and love of Christ in His wisdom. Ultimately, the sacred ear tempers pride with the humility of Christ.

---

75 Lewis, *Mere Christianity*, 112.

P.S. – To The Reader: Final Thoughts on the Sacred

Let me say here at the end, living a life without purpose makes about as much sense as putting ear drops in your pink eye, or eye drops in your pained ear. Beware of folly, foolishness, and embrace the fool's anti-dote, God's wisdom. The world seems a harsh place. Did you identify with the events, wars and the like, mentioned? The sacred ear bleeds compassion like Christ.

Did you think I was too harsh on the church? I almost left that section out, but feel that the sacred ear will push aside the selfish motives often trapped in churches and free us to serve Christ in obedience (*upakouo*) and joy. What about you, your *self* and, occasionally, selfishness? Does it affect your work, marriage, parenting, attitude, lack of silence, speech and foolishness in your own life? Do you see the importance of reflection, of practicing the art of the sacred ear so you can practice the presence of God that produces Christ-like actions?

Kathleen Norris tells the story of a Benedictine monk who had a pistol pulled on him. His reaction, his shock, his prayer led her to say "that there is no limit to the ways in which God might bring us to our senses, making us aware that it is time, and past time, to get on with it, to turn back, to return to the paths of righteousness."[76]

My prayer for you includes a prayer of sacred space–creating it daily as the practice of sacred silence, speech, and the art of the listening ear, so that you can value time, pursue God, hear Him, obey Him, and serve Him. I pray also God does not have to shock you by pistol or volcano or any other method to alarm your spiritual senses. Sacred space alone should cause you to seek God and enliven your spiritual senses.

Dear reader, I am almost done. Did you like the story about Mount St. Helen? Did you imagine the explosive lava, fire, ashes, soot, and devastation? Did your mind's eye imagine elk limping, dead fish washing up on the shores of the nearby lake, deer wailing, snow melting, trees falling on fire? Did your mind's eye capture the transformation from devastation to beauty: flowers in an array of Solomon's kingly clothing, the sun shining, trees dancing in the wind as they wave their arms and leaves, deer drinking from the lake without a

---

76 Kathleen Norris, *Amazing Grace: A Vocabulary of Faith* (New York: Riverhead Books, 1998), 230.

care in the world? Yes, dear reader, sacred space like Mount Saint Helen's nourishes, transforms, changes your life, and produces fruit and work beautiful to behold in God's eyes? May God give you a heart of grace, eyes to see His wonder, and ears to hear and obey Him each new day.

One of my favorite writers, Henri Nouwen, tells of a visit to the circus and especially the trapeze artists, the flyers and catchers who air to hand and hand to hand flew and captured each other as they "danced in the air."[77] Nouwen described the trapeze flyers in picturesque words, "They must brave the emptiness of space."[78] My prayer for you is that you will, with boldness, audacity, humility, and God's grace, brave the sacred space in the practice of the art of the sacred ear.

77　　　Henri Nouwen, *Turn My Mourning into Dancing: Moving through Hard Times with Hope* (Nashville, Tennessee: Thomas Nelson, 2001), 25.

78　　　Nouwen, *Turn My Mourning into Dancing*, 25.

Conclusion

When you read a book like *Sacred Space* you might feel overwhelmed, maybe burdened that you must do this, and yet wonder, "Who has the time? On the other hand, the time committed to sacred space will transform, enlighten, and challenge the soul in your walk with Christ. If you look at your calendar or your schedule implanted in your cell phone, you might feel like the sheep I talked about earlier in this book, sheep bottle-necked, trapped on London Bridge on a rainy day in rush hour traffic.

You might even feel like you want to stop everything, or at least slow your life down, and invoke the principles of sacred space into your life. Like the tourists in Westminster Abbey you might need to send yourself a message like the lady praying amid the chaos and tourism, "Shh-hhhhh! Be quiet. Be still. Practice sacred speech. Take some time and talk to Jesus." The psalmist says "Be still before the Lord and wait patiently for Him" (Psalm 37:4, *NIV*).

You might even wonder, "What will it take to dislodge the bottleneck, to escape the trap of pressured time, and to actually be still?" The sacred requires sacrifice (*sacrificium*). Paul wrote his *Letter to the Romans* to Christians also

surrounded by noise, chaos, and folly. While he in-
troduced the Gospel of Jesus as a remedy for righteousness, joy, and peace in their personal lives, he
also knew that the world they lived in like yours
demanded countless obligations of time, family,
work, and even political pressures that could be
as widespread as Roman power, Roman armies,
and Roman social expectations, or as narrow as
dealing with a client at work, what you might
call "office politics." Rome churned as an obligation society of pressure, politics, competition, and
compassion seldom hailed as a celebrated virtue
in the city center, marketplace, or *agora* where
people bought food and waited in lines to pay in a
kind of open air market.

Come to think of it, you live in a world
where time marches, pressure builds, and exhaustion attacks your heart, soul, mind, and emotions
like a boxer pummeling your gut. Come to think
of it your life churns, grinds, presses, claws, and
scratches you like a fingernail scraping a chalk
board. Come to think of it, your life looks like first-
century Rome: your world spinning as an obligation society of pressure, politics, competition, and
where compassion is seldom hailed as a celebrated virtue in the city center, marketplace, fast food

restaurant, freeway, or at the local grocery store where people purchase food and wait impatiently in long lines to pay or complain about the poor quality of food choices in an open air market. Not much has changed in the last two thousand years, has it?

Paul reminds Christians then as well as those today, "Therefore, I urge you, brothers, in view of God's mercy, to offer your bodies as living sacrifices, holy and pleasing to God—this is your spiritual act of worship. Do not conform any longer to the pattern of this world, but be transformed by the renewing of your mind. Then you will be able to test and approve what God's will is—his good, pleasing and perfect will" (Romans 12:1-2, *NIV*).

He calls for sacred silence, a target toward knowing God in His mercy and pleasure, desiring to please Him. Paul angles toward sacred speech, the two-sides of a coin faith that causes you to read the Scriptures and to pour out your heart to God, to speak to Him. Paul weaves a pattern in the world of obligations—marriage, school, work, financial, family, friendships, and the like, obligations that might deflate you, defeat you, and attempt to destroy you—and then Paul supplies strength for the journey: practice the art of the listening ear. The art of the listening ear helps you define, distinguish, and decide what priorities are important, how to spend your time, and what to cast aside, to throw out with the dung. Life's righteousness, joy, and peace might only come when you get rid of some stuff, offload the burdens, and cast your anxiety on Him because He cares for you (I Peter 5:7, *NIV*).

Paul also demonstrates one key to moving from noise to quiet, from chaos to peace, and from folly to wisdom: Present your bodies a living sacrifice. Paul indicates that you can conform to culture or you can conform to Christ. In conforming to Christ you present your body once and for all as a living sacrifice.

In ancient Judaism, Jews practiced worship of God, speaking, prayer, fasting, and almsgiving "in silence and in secret, and also without any recompense of reward."[79] In antiquity in Rome pagan sacrifices and rituals were practiced private and personal, as well as political and societal. Roman sacrifices were made public in public display in a temple, say, after a Roman conquest in war and in-

---

79   Guy G. Stroumsa, *The End of Sacrifice: Religious Transformations in Late Antiquity* (transl. by Susan Emanuel; Chicago: University of Chicago Press, 2009), 69.

cluded a celebration like a parade and ended with a sacrifice. Now Paul invited Roman Christian to sacrifice their own lives, metaphorically, practically, and personally.

Paul invites you to present your body as a living sacrifice, someone who will follow Christ, imitate Christ, serve Christ, and minister to others. He also encourages you to find solitude, peace, and wisdom in Christ. How can this be done? Try creating daily, weekly, monthly, even yearly extended times of sacred space. Sacred space implants the sacred in your heart, sacred quiet, peace, and wisdom that balances and builds your life toward a bold adventure.

Author's Final Note to the Reader

I hope you liked the book. I also pray that it helped you. I trust you will create sacred space in your own life. You can do this! Start today! Do not waste time! The Bible talks of time in two realms: *chronos* and *kairos*. *Chronos* is chronology, time as a place to be at a certain designated time, time as your crammed-packed schedule, time as the doctor's appointment, the drop off time for soccer practice, time as the calendar in your cell phone with alerts, or the time to start or end the work day. Does work ever end? Does time ever stop spinning and whirling? Does the merry go round ever come to a halt? *Chronos* keeps on ticking, pressuring, maybe frustrating if it is not tackled, controlled, prioritized.

Kairos is a season of time like fall, winter, spring, or summer. Seasons move slower, change and possess a value each on its own, say, falling colorful leaves golden yellow and red; cold fronts, north winds, and snowflakes tickling your nose; fresh flowers, birds singing, and life renewing itself from the dust of the earth and freshness of the morning air; and heat waves, a day at the beach, and illuminating sunsets. Remember that quote from Thoreau? "Morning air! If men will not drink at this fountainhead of the day..."[80] Ha! Thoreau also spoke about farming beans, "I was determined to know beans."[81]

Now I do not know a hill of beans about beans but I suggest you start your sacred space adventure in the morning. Start with ten minutes and increase it from there. Like kairos, a season of time, make it the only time of your day that you

---

80 Thoreau, *Walden*, 81.
81 Thoreau, *Walden*, 93.

do not rush. Be still. Know that He is God. Slow down. Slow time. Slow the mind, heart, and soul. Slow down and devour the morning air and drink in the Spirit of Christ. Enjoy sacred silence. Practice sacred speech. Reflect on Christ in sacred ear by listening. Do you hear his voice?

Old Hemingway was right, and I will paraphrase him here: "You must be prepared to work [practice sacred space] without applause."[82] Begin this process as soon as possible! Again I say, "You can do it!"

Or, since you know I like writers, Eudora Welty *On Writing* once said that if you are going to write you must stick your neck out.[83] Welty wrote, "No art ever came out of not risking your neck."[84] I bought that book in a country bookstore for two dollars in a small musty book shop in the back roads of Virginia on a trip. Dogs rested outside. A cool breeze soothed the morning air. And I paid cash, cold cash for that book! Of course, I only paid two dollars for it. Who finds a bargain like that? So, let me tell you, buy cheap books, old

82 Phillips, ed., *Ernest Hemingway on Writing*, 139.

83 Eudora Welty, *On Writing* (New York: Modern Library, 2002), 56.

84 Welty, *On Writing*, 56.

books, the best books in small bookshops, and pay cheap prices. Then quote the authors in books that have absolutely nothing to do with the book.

I am going to tell you a secret. I worked really hard to write this Eudora Welty quote in the book. It was not easy. Nothing in life worth doing will be easy! Quit looking for shortcuts! Start today. Practice sacred space! Because, to paraphrase Welty, "No sacred space ever came out of not risking your own neck."

So really, that is all I have to say about sacred space. Oh, I forgot to tell you about the weather. It is August here in Texas. Gray clouds puff in the sky with intermittent periods of sunshine. This morning I went to the pool as the sun peeked through these clouds. It was glorious. I heard birds singing. The sun looked marvelous when it peeked and winked at me. The air, the morning air, was crisp, not heavy or sticky or full of humidity like it can sometimes be here in Texas.

Now, present your bodies to God, practice sacred space, sacred silence, sacred speech, and the art of the sacred ear, and I promise you, you will feel alive, very alive, yes, very alive. Jesus said this would be true, "I have come that you might have life and have it to the full (John 10:10, *NIV*), or better yet, more abundantly!

Now that I have finished this book I think I will travel to London, maybe Cambridge, or Walden Pond in Massachusetts. Where I would really like to return to is that green porch swing in the mountains of North Carolina. Where I will most likely go is out on the back porch in my house here in Texas as the sun sets and practice sacred space. Join me. Come on!

Oh, the back porch provides picturesque sunsets. Red birds dart on the vines. Deer graze. And, low and behold, it's August and my backyard is still full of green grass. Usually, during this season (*kairos*), summer, my back yard is hard, brick-like and full of large splotches of yellow grass. Also, the vines radiate green. The grassy field and mesquite trees sway in the gentle breeze. Green leaves hang from the huge oak in my yard. I think it's over a hundred years old! It seems as if God the artist has finger-painted my backyard in August in Texas an array of colors! I wish the canvas could be transferred and hung on my refrigerator like a finger painting from a five year old. The beauty of my backyard right now is, for lack of a better term, majestic and miraculous. This is a miracle!

Practice sacred space and wait for the miracle to begin.

CPSIA information can be obtained
at www.ICGtesting.com
Printed in the USA
FFOW01n0619181116
29455FF